Beginning Primary Teaching

Beginning Primary Teaching:
Moving Beyond Survival

Angela Jacklin
Vivienne Griffiths and
Carol Robinson

Open University Press

Open University Press
McGraw-Hill Education
McGraw-Hill House
Shoppenhangers Road
Maidenhead
Berkshire
England
SL6 2QL

email: enquiries@openup.co.uk
world wide web: www.openup.co.uk

and Two Penn Plaza, New York, NY 10121-2289, USA

First published 2006

A catalogue record of this book is available from the British Library

ISBN 10: 0335 21908X (pb) 0335 219098 (hb)
ISBN 13: 9780335219087 (pb) 9780335219094 (hb)

Library of Congress Cataloging-in-Publication Data
CIP data applied for

Typeset by YHT Ltd
Printed in Poland by OZGraf S.A.
www.polskabook.pl

Contents

List of figures and tables

Figures

Tables

Foreword

This pioneering book on teachers' early career learning provides a rich account of how primary school teachers engage in learning as a natural response to the problems they encounter in and beyond their classrooms. This account is based on several pieces of research conducted by the authors over a seven year period with recently qualified teachers. While much of their account is specific to teachers, it also matches research undertaken by myself and others in a range of different professions in three important respects: such learning is mainly informal; much of it is significantly affected by workplace climate and relationships; and its magnitude is much greater than most people recognize. Their research programme found both similarities and differences in the way that primary school teachers approach their learning, and in how their learning is supported and/or constrained by people and circumstances.

However, it is not just the research that is novel. The structure and mode of presentation of this book contribute even more to its pioneering character. The changing experiences and perspectives of the teachers who were engaged in this research are not only the subject of this book but also its substance. These teachers have the dominant voice, especially in the first half of the book. Four ongoing case studies of learning during the first three years of four newly qualified teachers from different backgrounds run throughout the book; and their voices are supplemented by the views of a wider group of teachers who were also interviewed on several occasions. Finally evidence of the relative frequency of particular views and experiences is provided by quantitative data from nearly 350 questionnaires.

Unusually early career teachers are the prime audience for this book. It is directly addressed to them and structured to help them to reflect on and plan their own learning with greater awareness of possible courses of action and informed by the experiences of other teachers at the same stage and in similar circumstances. Not only does it offer vicarious learning from their colleagues who participated in the research, but it also discusses their own learning agenda and suggests ways in which they might evaluate it, extend it or prioritize within it. The book is an excellent example of how the findings of research can be authentically presented to teachers and made relevant to their current needs and concerns.

The second intended audience for this book comprises those working within or outside the school who are in a position through closeness of contact or formal role to support (or fail to support) teachers' learning. For them the first important message is to listen to the teachers' voices and try to understand each teacher's individual perspective. Secondly they need to understand the balance of factors affecting each teacher's learning and, where necessary, intervene to extend the range of learning opportunities or make it easier for teachers to take up existing opportunities. This could include giving feedback which recognizes their progress and helps them to understand some of their more challenging concerns.

The book is divided into four parts. Part 1 is chronologically focused, and concentrates on the basic issues dominating teachers' concerns over their first three years. The evidence is drawn mainly from the evidence of the first four case study teachers. It covers getting their first job; the initial shock of taking on 'real responsibility' (nurses undergo a very similar experience); gaining confidence and learning to manage their time (also true of other professions); their planned development of professional knowledge at work; and becoming a 'real teacher' (a critical aspect of developing a professional identity). It concludes with teachers' accounts of their professional development over this three year period and their gradual take up of additional responsibilities within the school.

Part 2 looks in detail at how new teachers handled what were generally perceived to be their four main challenges: learning to plan and prepare their teaching and still have a life; expanding their subject competence beyond the basics to cover the rest of the primary curriculum; issues linked to working with pupils individually and in groups, including the handling of diversity, behaviour management and assessment; and working with adults such as mentors, teacher colleagues, teaching assistants and parents. These accounts demonstrate to those who believe that competence can be achieved at the time of qualification just how much further learning is needed during those first three years.

Part 3 builds on Part 2 and introduces further data to analyse professional learning at a more general level. This discussion is focused around two learning models, both starting with *survival* followed by *coping*. Learning teaching skills then proceeds through *exploration* to *proficiency*, while learning other professional skills such as preparation, time management and working with parents, proceeds through *realism* to *balance*. This recognizes that these wider professional roles have to be managed to avoid levels of work incompatible with any reasonable work–life balance. These models are then used to help teachers evaluate their areas of strength and needs for further learning; and to encourage them to develop their own 'realistic' professional development strategy.

Part 4 concludes the book with a look five years into the future. The first look is through the eyes of the contributing teachers, whose perspectives are then used to prompt readers to consider their own thoughts about their future and about what professional learning they might need to reach their desired goal. The second look is based on the implications of three current policy initiatives: school and workforce remodelling, interschool networks for exchanging experience and the move towards cross-professional children's services. All will involve teachers in new thinking and new ways of working.

Professor Michael Eraut,
University of Sussex

Preface

The ideas for this book arose directly from our work as teacher educators at the University of Sussex and from our interest in the early career development of primary teachers. Over a number of years we have been researching aspects of professional development and learning. At first we focused on our own trainee teachers, during their initial training and, more recently, on their first years in teaching. Following funding from the Economic and Social Research Council (ESRC), we were able to look more broadly at the preparedness and professional development of beginning primary teachers in three local education authorities (LEAs). As a result of the findings of this research, we then became involved in a number of LEA funded projects which enabled us to develop emerging ideas further. These included an evaluation of a pilot project on early professional development and an investigation into the retention of mid-career teachers.

The model which underpins much of the work in this book arose initially from the ESRC funded project. It has since been developed, adapted and refined in a number of contexts, for example with teachers trained on employment-based routes. In addition the model has proved useful in our work with teaching assistants, helping us to understand the development of their professional role and for some, helping us to understand their transition into teaching.

More recently research has demonstrated the importance of the early years of teaching, particularly in terms of retention. Moreover, it has become clear that, despite the support and funding available in a teacher's induction year, teachers' early career development remains a relatively neglected area. In particular there is a lack of support materials aimed at this group of teachers, a gap which prompted us to write this book. We hope that new teachers and those who work with them will find it a useful resource.

Angela Jacklin,
Vivienne Griffiths and
Carol Robinson

Acknowledgements

We would like to thank all those who contributed in so many ways to the development of this book, especially the new and early career primary teachers who took part in our interviews, responded to our questionnaires and were so open about their experiences in teaching. In particular we would like to thank Jackie Barrett, Juliet Hammond, Corinne Pepper and Tina Potter who, together with a number of other beginning teachers, remained so willing to work with us over a number of years. We are very appreciative of their continued involvement and the way in which they helped us to shape our ideas, which in turn shaped the book itself.

The research which underpins this book was funded from a number of sources, including the Economic and Social Research Council, which provided the funding for the main research project (R000223489), and the local education authorities with whom we worked. We are grateful to them all for their support. In addition thanks are extended to a number of our colleagues at the University of Sussex School of Education, especially Professor Michael Eraut, for their suggestions, support and critical engagement with the ideas and with the text. We would also like to thank Maddy Robbins who helped in the preparation of the manuscript.

List of abbreviations

AfL	Assessment for learning
AST	Advanced skills teacher
CPD	Continuing professional development
DfEE	Department for Education and Employment
DfES	Department for Education and Skills
DT	Design and technology
EAL	English as an additional language
EPD	Early professional development
ESRC	Economic and Social Research Council
GTC	General Teaching Council
GTP	Graduate Teacher Programme
HLTA	Higher level teaching assistant
ICT	Information and communication technology
IEP	Individual education plan
ITE	Initial teacher education
ITT	Initial teacher training
LEA	Local education authority
LSA	Learning support assistant
NCSL	National College for School Leadership
NLS	National Literacy Strategy
NNS	National Numeracy Strategy
NQT	Newly qualified teacher
Ofsted	Office for Standards in Education
PE	Physical education
PGCE	Postgraduate Certificate in Education
PPA	Planning, preparation and assessment
QTS	Qualified teacher status
RE	Religious education
RTP	Registered Teacher Programme
SATs	Standard Assessment Tasks
SEN	Special educational needs
SENCO	Special educational needs coordinator
TA	Teaching assistant
TTA	Teacher Training Agency

Introduction

How will I get through the first term?
How will I survive?
Who can I go to for help?

This book engages with these and similar questions which are often in the minds of teachers as they start out in their new careers. It does so by drawing on the voices of beginning primary teachers. The aim of the book is to support teachers' early professional development and learning. In addition, it aims to provide a teaching and learning resource for professionals working with early career teachers.

Four case studies of beginning primary teachers are at the heart of the book. Abbey, Cathryn, Fatou and Gina are introduced in the first chapter and what happened to them during their first three years in teaching gradually unfolds. Their experiences are used as a way of illustrating and exploring the early years of teaching. In essence, the book is about teachers like these four. Through their experiences and those of other early career teachers, the book aims to help new teachers to reflect on their own practice. It also aims to enable teachers to relate to and reflect on the experiences of others, thus providing practical professional support throughout the important early years of their careers.

Throughout the book we have included a number of activities which are used to help the reader think about their practice and reflect on ways of addressing challenges they may encounter. The activities are also used to help prepare the reader for situations they may meet for the first time, as well as to give practical examples of how other new teachers have dealt with similar situations. Throughout the book the voices of new teachers are drawn upon to illustrate and explain some of the experiences of beginning teachers at key stages in their early career.

The book is based on three main research projects, details of which may be found in the Appendix. In addition we have drawn on findings from a number of smaller research projects with which we have been involved. Although the four case studies that feature throughout the book are all of women teachers, this is incidental. They were selected because together they represent a range of key issues, critical incidents and experiences which emerged from the research projects.

The vast majority of teachers involved in our research were female (89 percent of the total respondents), reflecting the predominance of women in primary teaching, an imbalance that recruitment strategies are seeking to redress (see www.tta.gov.uk). Although the quotations that we use in the book include some from men as well as women teachers, we do not identify or name anyone other than the four case study teachers and gender-free language has been used throughout the book.

The structure of the book

The book is divided into four parts:

1   Early experiences of teaching
2   Key issues and problems: moving beyond survival
3   Reflecting on practice: towards a model of professional learning
4   Looking ahead

Part 1 introduces the book and the four case study teachers: Abbey, Cathryn, Fatou and Gina. It describes what happened to these four teachers in the first three years of their teaching career, highlighting key points and issues arising during this period, for instance, obtaining their first teaching post and their experiences during their first term in teaching.

Part 2 of the book identifies and tackles some of the more common issues and challenges which new teachers often face in their early careers. Many of these issues and challenges will have been illustrated in the first part of the book through the experiences of the four teachers. However, in this second part of the book, a more in-depth look is taken at these issues and challenges, and ways of tackling them are discussed by drawing on the experiences and perspectives of a larger group of new teachers of which Abbey, Cathryn, Fatou and Gina were a part.

Part 3 introduces a model of professional learning which is used to help describe and explain what happened to Abbey, Cathryn, Fatou and Gina during their early careers. The model is also used to help the reader to reflect on their own professional practice and learning, as well as their stages in professional development. Major factors affecting early professional learning are explored, specifically in relation to the acquisition of teaching skills and coping with professional demands. Part 3 also raises and discusses issues of retention in relation to teachers' early careers.

Part 4 looks ahead in two ways, individually in terms of teachers' career and professional development, and more widely in terms of the changing landscape of teaching and the role of primary teachers.

Who is this book for?

This book is primarily for beginning teachers in primary education: that is, those completing initial teacher training, newly qualified and early career teachers. It will have relevance to all new teachers, including the growing number entering teaching through employment-based routes, such as the Graduate Teacher Programme (GTP). The structure and content of the book is written in a direct and accessible style which we hope you will find easy to read.

This book is also for teacher educators in higher education to support trainees' transition into the induction year. In addition, this book will be useful for induction mentors in schools and local education authority personnel, who will be able to use the book in providing school-based support for early professional development.

PART 1
Early experiences of teaching

The first part of this book is based mainly on the experiences of four newly qualified teachers, Abbey, Cathryn, Fatou and Gina, chosen to illustrate the experiences of beginning primary teachers. As we look chronologically at what happened to them during their first three years in their new careers, we focus in particular on key transition points. We look at how the teachers moved from initial training into their first teaching post as well as what happened during their first term in teaching. We explore the 'reality shock' of their first job, taking full responsibility for a class and what it means to become, as the teachers described, a 'real' teacher. We also look at the ways in which the four new teachers gradually gained confidence, took on more responsibility within the school and learnt to manage their time and the professional demands of teaching during their first three years.

Throughout this first part of the book we draw mainly on the voices of these four case study teachers, Abbey, Cathryn, Fatou and Gina, as we uncover what happened to them during their first three years. However, we will also focus on findings from in-depth interviews with a further 30 newly qualified teachers (27 women and 3 men). This total sample (of 34) represented a cross-section of teachers from a larger group which we introduce in Part 2 of the book. The sample included a range of people in terms of age, gender, type of initial training, type of school (rural/urban, size, age-phase, etc.), prior work experience and specialist key stage. All 34 teachers completed questionnaires after their first term and after their first year in teaching. They were also interviewed towards the end of their first year in teaching, and again near the beginning of their second year. Additional interviews were carried out with the four case study teachers in their fourth year of teaching (see Study 1 in the Appendix for further details). Following up the teachers' questionnaire responses, the interviews with the 34 teachers at the end of their first year and beginning of their second year covered the following areas:

- *General information about NQTs' teaching position*: location of school, age group taught, areas of responsibility if any.
- *Experiences of the first year in teaching, with a particular focus on the first term*: hours of work, workload, highs and lows.
- *The rewards and challenges experienced by teachers in their first year(s) of teaching*: e.g. the reward of children making progress compared to the challenge of dealing with difficult behaviour in the classroom.
- *Best or least well prepared subject areas and other aspects of school life*: e.g. most prepared in teaching core subjects compared to least prepared in working with other adults in the classroom.
- *School expectations*: details of lesson planning, assessment, etc. required by the headteacher or senior management.
- *Support from school, LEA, friends*: where support was strongest and where it was lacking.
- *Futures*: where they saw themselves in five years' time and why.

For a beginning teacher the move from training into teaching can be an especially difficult time. A number of factors, for example the role of the headteacher and relationships with staff, pupils and parents, can affect the success of their first steps in this new career. The first part of this book highlights these factors through the experiences of the four case study teachers. It is hoped that you will be able to identify with the experiences described, and apply them directly to your own contexts.

1
Getting your first job

This chapter will focus on the period of transition from initial teacher training into the first teaching post. It starts by introducing four teachers who were about to begin their new career in teaching. Drawing on the case studies of these four teachers' experiences, the chapter will consider such aspects as how trainee teachers apply and obtain their first appointments, preparation for the new job and their feelings during this interim period. We will look at the motivations, apprehensions and prior experiences of the case study teachers. The chapter will end by looking at the role played by the school in helping the new teachers to settle in during the first weeks.

Introduction

In this chapter we will introduce you to four new teachers: Abbey, Cathryn, Fatou and Gina. Just like these four teachers, those of you who are now starting out in teaching will have trained on one of a number of initial teacher training programmes. We will consider the training programmes which the new teachers have followed and will also consider the individual personal circumstances of each of these four teachers. In particular, this chapter will focus on the motivations and apprehensions of these teachers during the period of transition from initial teacher training to their first teaching post. It is likely that you will be able to relate to some of their experiences.

Regardless of which training route you followed, in order to become a qualified teacher in England you are required to have a degree and to have achieved the standards required for qualified teacher status (DfES/TTA 2003). It may be that you followed a BA, BEd or BSc programme with training for qualified teacher status built into the degree programme. Or, if you already had a degree, it is likely that you followed either a Post Graduate Certificate in Education (PGCE) programme, or a Graduate Teacher Programme (GTP). The GTP is an employment-based route into teaching which an increasing number of trainees, in particular mature entrants, are choosing to follow. A smaller number of you may have completed the Registered Teacher

Programme (RTP), an employment-based route which allows you to complete your degree while training to be a teacher.

Introducing Abbey, Cathryn, Fatou and Gina

Let's meet the four new teachers.

First, Abbey. As Abbey said, 'I'd always wanted to teach but I kind of dropped out of school, I never actually did A levels, so I worked and studied alongside my job until I took the teacher training course'. When Abbey left school she worked as a clerical officer for a few years and during that time realized that in order to get into teaching she would need to gain additional qualifications. She applied locally for a place on a teacher training course and was accepted onto a primary BA qualified teacher status (QTS) programme. She was in her mid-20s when she graduated.

Cathryn, second, also followed a BA (QTS) programme but was older than Abbey; she was in her mid-30s when she graduated. She had young children, and before training as a teacher, she had been working as a classroom assistant in her children's school. Cathryn explained: 'When I was a classroom assistant, everyone said to me I should be a teacher. I'd never really thought about it, but then decided I should give it a go, because I do like working with children'.

The third teacher is Fatou who, like Cathryn, was in her mid-30s when she qualified and had also been a teaching assistant in her children's school. Unlike Abbey and Cathryn, Fatou's route into teaching was through the GTP. She said: 'When I was a classroom assistant, I was able to study part-time for my degree and then I was hoping to do a PGCE: I just liked being in the classroom, being with the children. I'd been studying for six years and got a degree in Professional Educational Studies, but then I couldn't get on the PGCE course because I didn't have an actual subject area.' You may have experienced similar problems. Unless you have a degree in a recognized National Curriculum subject you may have had difficulty in being accepted on to a PGCE programme.

Gina was the eldest of the four teachers. She came relatively late to teaching, following a PGCE programme in her mid-40s. She had started work as a bank clerk and then had had a family. She explained how she moved into teaching: 'It was when my eldest son was 5; I started to go into school to help as a parent helper. My son's now 17, so it's taken me a long time. I've got three children and I'd helped out in school on and off with all three. I just decided I wanted to do it. All my family are teachers and I suppose I sort of kicked against it. But I was a parent helper ... I knew I just wanted to teach.' Unable to get a place on a PGCE programme locally, she applied more widely and was accepted on a programme some distance away. Not wanting to uproot her family, Gina decided to live away for part of each week to allow her to complete the PGCE programme.

> I'd worked for nine years ... it had been a long journey. I'd done a degree with the Open University; I started that when my first son was 18 months, then I'd gone away for a year to do my PGCE in Dorset. I used to travel down on Monday and come back Friday, so I had put a lot in to get where I was.

Abbey, Cathryn, Fatou and Gina were starting out in teaching with a range of different life experiences as well as school and training experiences. We chose these four teachers from a large group of new teachers with whom we had conducted in-depth interviews, asking about their initial training and teaching. Their experiences in their early teaching careers illustrate the range of issues and concerns expressed by many of the beginning teachers to whom we spoke. You will meet each of these four teachers again in the next three chapters and again at various points throughout the book as we follow their development through the early part of their teaching career.

The first teaching appointment

In this section we will look at how Abbey, Cathryn, Fatou and Gina obtained their first teaching posts and how they felt about making the transition from trainee teacher to teacher.

Abbey talked about how she obtained her first teaching post and how she felt at the time.

> I remember being very excited, absolutely delighted ... I'd gone through the teaching pool through [an LEA] and then I just got a call from the head of the school saying there was a post going at the school. It was actually the same day as I'd arranged to go and see another school, so I looked round both schools and decided not to apply for the other job, so I didn't even have to have another interview.

Abbey was clear that she only wanted to work within one specific local education authority (LEA). She was very excited once she'd got her first appointment. There are different ways in which you can obtain your first teaching post. Some of the new teachers to whom we spoke had applied to lots of schools in different areas, while others had chosen to restrict themselves to one locality. Some of the new teachers chose to work part-time, some took short-term contracts and some worked in a variety of schools on a supply basis. They wanted to experience a range of different teaching situations which they felt would enable them to make a more informed choice about the type of school in which they would like to work on a more permanent basis.

A small number of new teachers who applied for, but did not get, permanent teaching posts also found themselves with short-term contracts or a range of supply posts. Although initially disappointing, this varied experience could be very positive. Abbey was very pleased because she hadn't had to apply for lots of jobs but had got her first teaching post relatively quickly through the LEA's teaching 'pool'. The teaching pool system is a way in which some LEAs recruit a selection of new teachers. The teachers apply to the LEA itself and have a pool interview, which is usually taken by LEA staff and headteachers who are looking to appoint a newly qualified teacher to their own schools. Not all LEAs operate a pool system, and among those LEAs that do, there are variations, but broadly the aim is to smooth the process of matching newly qualified teachers with schools wanting to recruit.

Cathryn's situation was very different from that of Abbey's: although both of them applied to an LEA teaching pool, Cathryn specifically wanted to remain in one geographical area and was restricted to applying to one LEA. She was a mature student with family commitments and had previously been a teaching assistant in one of the local schools.

> I went back to the school where I'd been a teaching assistant, so I knew everybody; we're like a little family so I didn't have that stress on myself of having to get to know everybody. You see, I'd gone in as a parent helper when my son was younger and then I became a teaching assistant and one day the head said to me, 'You're wasting yourself, you could be a teacher'; and so I applied to do the course and I had support because another colleague was doing the same course and she lived nearby so we used to travel together. Then when I'd finished the course, I'd been for the pool interview and passed that, then the head of the school where I'd been a teaching assistant rang me up and said about the job at her school.

After Cathryn was accepted by the teaching pool, she was contacted by the head of the school where she had previously worked as a teaching assistant. Similar to Abbey, Cathryn obtained her first teaching post without having to apply for too many jobs. Before starting she was a little anxious because she was not fully confident that others in the school would view her as a teacher now, and no longer a teaching assistant. She explained:

> At first I thought, 'I don't know'. I wasn't sure if I'd be accepted back at the school; I didn't know how the staff would see me, if they'd see me as a teacher. But I've had support from the staff and for me it's been perfect.

In some respects, Fatou was in a similar situation to Cathryn, having to make the transition from teaching assistant to teacher within the same school. However, for Fatou this transition was made during her training year rather than her induction year.

Having followed a GTP route, Fatou was in a different position from Abbey and Cathryn when it came to obtaining her first teaching post because GTP trainees are employed by the school while they train. She continued to be employed in the same school, only now as a qualified teacher.

> It must be really strange if you move to another school; I didn't want that. This job is on my doorstep, I like the staff, I like the children. I've got no reason to move and I stayed with the same year group, so I had no planning to do, I'd done it all in my GTP year.

Not all teachers trained on the GTP automatically obtain a post in the school in which they have trained, and there is no obligation on the school to continue the contract beyond the training year. However in Fatou's case there was a vacancy and the school was able to give her a contract as a qualified teacher. Fatou's transition from the role of trainee teacher to that of qualified teacher was also relatively smooth. Not only was she in the same school for both her training and her newly qualified teacher (NQT) years, she was also teaching a Year 2 class for the second year running.

> Because of my training, it was slightly different for me as I did the GTP, so I'd trained for a year in the class, so the transition from ITT [initial teacher training] to actually teaching didn't seem to be much different, it just seemed to flow. When I started my training, I started in the September and I was training and teaching from the start, but once I was in my NQT year I actually had more time as I have non-contact time, whereas in my non-contact time when I was training I was at college.

As a mature student, Gina had local commitments and was restricted to working in a particular area, especially as she had spent the last year away from home training. She was initially concerned about what other people had said to her, implying that she might have difficulties when competing for a teaching post with younger new teachers. However this concern was unfounded, as Gina did not experience problems in getting her first appointment.

> I'd had an interview with the LEA pool and passed that, then didn't hear anything for months, but as I wasn't the main bread winner and I hadn't been working before that it wasn't too bad. I think I had my interview for the pool in April and then it wasn't until July that the

head of a school rang me up, they'd lost my details. But I went to the school that day for an interview and they offered me the job. It was a bit further than I'd wanted to travel. It takes about 20 minutes, but it's a lovely school and I'd really wanted Reception or Year 1 and I was going to be teaching Year 2, but that didn't matter too much. It was a sigh of relief.

When you are applying for jobs, lots of people will give you advice and helpful hints. Sometimes however, as in Gina's case, advice may not always be accurate or concerns substantiated. Check the source of the advice and 'helpful' comments you are given. Some of them may be valid, for example teachers' union publications or LEA advice, but some may simply be hearsay. You will need to make your own decisions about whether or not you take notice of what others say to you.

Getting your first job

When applying for your first teaching post, think about what is important to you. For example, is the geographical location of the school important? Is the year group you are going to teach important to you? Do you mind what type of school you teach in, for instance, whether it's large or small? Will you mind if it's an open plan school? You need to think carefully about what *you* want from your teaching post.

In the following two quotes, the teachers to whom we spoke knew what they needed to do to get a job in which they would be happy. The first teacher knew there would be a lot of pressure because of being restricted to applying for posts in one town and knowing competition would be tough. The teacher was clear about what kind of school they wanted to teach in and was therefore well placed to apply for teaching posts early. The second teacher was also restricted to applying for posts in one area and also wanted to work in a particular type of school. This teacher's strategy for finding a job was different, deciding to go on supply initially to allow time to become more familiar with schools in the area.

There weren't a great deal of jobs in [a specific town], or rather there were a huge amount of people applying for the jobs that were there. There was pressure to get a job really quickly, but I was lucky, I managed to get a job in a school I really wanted to be in and in a school which was only 5 minutes away from where I lived and I totally love my school. I would have looked further afield but I really wanted to be near home. I didn't want to spend half an hour or three-quarters of an hour travelling to school.

I decided to do supply teaching for one term so then I could see different schools and get an idea about the type of school I wanted to work in and my plan worked brilliantly. I found out exactly the type of school I wanted to work in. I knew I didn't want an open-plan school, and I wanted a school where the staff work together.

The two teachers above had clear criteria about what they wanted from their first teaching post, but they applied different strategies. The following teacher left applying for a job until much later due to lack of confidence in their ability to teach.

I left searching for a job until quite late as I didn't have the confidence at first. The thing was, my first placement was really difficult. I had one very violent child, and I hardly taught during the placement. The class teacher was with me all the time, she hardly let me teach … [My tutor] was brilliant, she gave me loads of advice about different behavioural techniques. Then, I had a fantastic mentor in my second placement. I mean, in the first week, she let me make all my mistakes, and I made every mistake possible! Then she said, 'Right, let's go over the week and talk about it'. I knew I'd made the mistakes and she said, 'Well, you know where you're going wrong, and how to put things right, so let's make this our starting point', and that was great, she was really fantastic. So I got more confidence in my second placement, but left looking for a job 'til near the end of the placement.

Remember, you've worked hard to get this far through your initial training, so have confidence: go for it, apply for jobs in schools where you think you will be happy. Activity 1.1 below will help you to determine the criteria that are important to you when deciding which teaching posts to apply for.

Activity 1.1

Think about what is important to you when applying for a teaching post. This may include location, type of school (e.g. phase or open-plan, etc.), size of school, age group/key stage, etc. Write down everything that you think is important.

Now look at what you have written and weigh each item in order of importance, spending some time thinking about what really is important to you and why.

Now do the same in relation to what you know you don't want. What couldn't you cope with?

The ideas included in the two lists you have written will help you determine which posts are suitable for you and which are not. Once you have decided to apply for a job, the next step is to complete the application form and hopefully attend for interview. The information included in Figures 1.1 and 1.2 below may be of help to you when writing application forms and preparing for interviews.

When completing application forms consider the following:

1   Look closely at the job description and decide whether you really want to apply for the job. Are you prepared? Could you do what the school/LEA wants of you? Is it what *you* want?

2   Having decided to apply for the post, think about your strengths and your experience to date. How do they complement what the school/LEA requires of you?

3   Complete the application form, giving details of your strengths and experience.

4   When completing the section which allows you to write freely about yourself, ensure that you address the areas specifically mentioned in the job description and add other areas according to your strengths and interests.

5   If there are any areas of the application form or job description which you are unsure about, contact the school/LEA and ask about them.

6   Keep a copy of your application form as this may help when completing other application forms. Also, if invited for interview, you may wish to read the application form to remind you of what you had written.

7   It is up to you as an individual to decide how early you start applying for teaching posts. However, for peace of mind, it may be better to start applying early, in particular if you are limiting your applications to a particular geographical area or to a particular type of school.

Figure 1.1   The application form

Hopefully you will be short-listed for interview at one or more of the schools to which you have applied. It is usual for teachers to be interviewed by a panel. In a school the panel is likely to comprise the headteacher, members of the school's senior management team, school governors and, increasingly as part of the interview day, pupils from the school council who will also want to ask you questions. If you are involved in an LEA pool interview, LEA staff, headteachers and school governors are likely to be on the interview panel; however, it is unlikely that pupils will form part of this panel. You may be feeling a little anxious about the interview, especially if you have had limited experience of interviews. Figure 1.2 includes some ideas for you to think about before attending for an interview.

Before the interview, consider the following:

1   Be sure you know exactly where the school is and arrive on time.

2   Don't forget during the interview, as well as the school/LEA wanting to know if you would be suitable for the post they have advertised, *you* also want to know that this is a school/LEA in which you are going to be able to work and be happy. Prepare some questions in advance that address the areas you would like to know more about.

3   During the actual interview listen to the questions asked and answer them as fully as possible. If necessary, ask the interviewer to repeat the question.

4   If you have started building a portfolio of your experiences and achievements, take that along to the interview.

5   Towards the end of the interview it is normal for a member of the panel to ask if you have any further questions. If some of your questions have not been answered, now is the time to ask them. Think about whether the questions you would like answered are general, or if you would like to address them to particular members of the interview panel.

Figure 1.2   The interview

Settling into their first teaching post

Schools help new teachers to settle into life in school in a variety of ways. Often, having obtained their first teaching posts, new teachers are invited into school by the headteacher. This is usually the first step in the settling in process and provides an opportunity to meet your new colleagues and to begin to find out about life in your new school. For Cathryn and also for Fatou, they were already familiar with the staff and school from previous employment. Their concerns were more to do with acceptance of their change of role, rather than with settling into a new environment. However, Abbey and Gina were both starting at schools of which they had no prior knowledge. Settling in takes longer when things are less familiar, as you will probably have experienced when you started new teaching placements. How did Abbey and Gina deal with this?

Abbey spent time in her new school at the end of the school year immediately after graduating. Her school offered this opportunity and Abbey made the effort to ensure she was able to take advantage of this. She learnt a great deal from these few weeks as she explains:

> I spent a few days with the other teacher in my year group. She helped me quite a bit, we did the planning together. Altogether I spent about 2 to 3 weeks in the schools in June and July. I could choose how much time I spent there, but I decided to spend a lot of time there, so I got to know the staff and I was shown all of the programmes of study, the resources and just spent the time generally getting to know how the school operated.

Many teachers obtain their first post in a school which is new to them. Sometimes the headteacher will invite you to spend time in the school, however, not all may do this. You should not be afraid of asking if you can visit the school before actually starting your new post. Any time you spend in school is valuable, as Abbey discovered. Remember this is for real now: you are the teacher and although people will be there to support you, you have overall responsibility for your class and there is a lot to find out.

Gina's situation was very different from Abbey's. Gina did not have the same opportunity to visit the school over a period of time or talk to colleagues to the same extent as Abbey prior to starting her post in September. As a result of this, it was not possible for some of the questions Gina had about her new post to be answered and some concerns grew, especially in relation to how to plan for her new class. When talking about contact with staff from the school, she explained:

> I had no contact over the summer. I'd had a meeting at the end of July with a couple of the teachers. I think the planning was my main worry and really it's taken years for it to come clear and I think there wasn't enough about it on the course. I used to think, 'How do I plan lessons?' I used to sit for hours 'til midnight planning for the next day. It has become clearer and easier over time.

Once you have been successful in gaining your first teaching post, you can begin to think about the process of settling into the school. Activity 1.2 below will help you think about what you can do and what your school can do to help with this process.

Activity 1.2

Think about ways in which your new school can help you to settle in. What do you need to find out about your new school before you actually start teaching? Make a list. You may include questions such as which classroom you will be teaching in. You may want copies of the school's various subject strategies and school policies. Who do you think you should try to meet? Why?

What do you think you need to do and what questions would you like answered? Refer to Figure 1.3 which will give you some ideas to start you off. You will probably find that you will want to add to your list after you have made an initial visit to the school, so a good idea is to write the list in a notebook which you can take with you into school.

Now you have your list, think about how you are going to deal with it. Not all your questions will be answered during your first visit. Prioritize questions which are important to you and think about who can help answer these. Remember your new colleagues won't be available during all of the holidays as they will have their own commitments.

Thinking about your new school, you will be:

- meeting new colleagues;

- meeting the children – your new class;

- finding out about school routines and procedures;

- seeing your new classroom;

- finding out what resources are available to you: in your classroom, within the year group, department, curriculum area and school;

- finding out about areas of responsibility. What will the school expect of you?

- identifying what curriculum plans are in place for your class;

- finding out about school policies; and

- finding out if there is anyone you can contact over the holidays before you start your post: you may have concerns you would like to talk through with someone.

Figure 1.3 Settling into school life

Advice for NQTs applying for posts now

When Abbey, Cathryn, Fatou and Gina were asked what advice they would give to NQTs when applying for their first teaching posts, they said:

> I'd say definitely go and spend some time in the school and when you are applying for the job, make sure you know something about the school and what it's like. I know you're desperate to get a job but every school feels different and all staff are different and you've got to be in a school where you feel comfortable.
>
> (Abbey)

> If you are an NQT who has just been to college, be prepared to think, 'I don't know it all' and have confidence because children will soon pick up if you haven't got confidence, they will know if you're weak. You also need to be enthusiastic.
>
> (Cathryn)

> They've got to realize that what you do as an NQT, you will learn more than you have done at university.
>
> (Fatou)

> I'd just tell them that the planning will slot into place. Don't worry about it too much, it's just a question of time and it will all come together.
>
> (Gina)

Key findings and action points

This chapter has focused on two key issues faced by new teachers when getting their first teaching post:

- applying for your first post
- settling into your first school

Applying for your first teaching post can be exciting and rewarding, but also a little daunting at the same time. You will need to decide certain criteria that are important to you when choosing which jobs to apply for. This will depend largely on your personal circumstances and whether you are limited to applying to a relatively small geographical area. The interview is an important part of the application process both for you and for the school/LEA. It gives both parties the opportunity to find out more about each other. Use this opportunity to ask questions about the school/LEA to which you are applying. It is important that you work in a school/LEA which suits you and your preferences.

Once you have obtained your first teaching post, whether you have a temporary or permanent, a part-time or full-time contract, you will need to give some thought to how the school can help you, and how you can help yourself settle into your new school. The more you can prepare for your teaching post before you actually start teaching, the more confident you are likely to feel.

Action points

- When applying for your first teaching post think carefully about what you want from it. What *must* the post be able to offer you? What would you *ideally like* the post to offer? What would you *not* want the post to include? Once you have answered these questions, ensure that the job you are applying for matches your preferences.
- Having obtained your first teaching post, decide what you need to find out about your new school prior to actually starting to teach there. You may not be able to find out everything you want to know. If you list what you *need* to find out, what you *would like* to find out before you actually start teaching there and what you *could* find out at a later date, this will help you prioritize your needs. From this you can work out who could help you with the areas you need to know about before you start teaching at the school.

Concluding discussion

Throughout this chapter we have outlined the experiences of four teachers as they moved from their initial teacher training programme into their first teaching post. Each of these teachers had different personal circumstances which to some extent affected the teaching posts for which they applied. There are several factors to consider when applying for your first teaching post. The ideas given in Figures 1.2 and 1.3 will help you with this process and will help you determine what is important to you.

If you are going to a school where you have previously been a teaching assistant, a parent helper or where you have been on teaching practice as part of your initial teacher training programme, you are likely to find that your transition into teaching will be relatively smooth. You will already be familiar with the school building and ethos, the teaching staff, the pupils and the parents, and you will be familiar with the environment which you are about to enter. If, however, you are starting at a completely new school, you will find it helpful to spend time in the school, particularly with the members of staff you are likely to be working with, before actually starting to teach there.

2
Surviving the first term

The first term in teaching is a crucial one in terms of the beginning teacher's survival. Newly qualified teachers need to settle in very quickly and establish themselves with their new class. In this chapter the case studies will be used to paint a vivid picture of the early weeks of the first term and illustrate some of the main problems and issues faced by beginning teachers. The current range of routes into teaching now provides the new teacher with a variety of strengths, skills and challenges. These will be explored through the case studies, and you will be encouraged to relate them to your own experiences.

Introduction

Well, this is what it has all been for. You are now a fully fledged teacher and about to set off on what will be an exciting early career – your first term with your very own class. What will this first term hold for you? When you look back at the end of term, what will you remember most about it?

Maybe you have already started your first job and you are reading this chapter part-way through your first year or just before starting your second year. This chapter is also for you. You will find that there is much you can learn from thinking about and reflecting on your experiences, and this reflection will help you when you come to start work with your new class. Although the reflective activities are mainly written for new teachers, we have included variations, where appropriate, for those with more teaching experience which you can easily adapt to your own situation.

As we will stress on a number of occasions in this book, reflecting on what we are doing and have done is crucial to improving our practice (see also Pollard 2002a, b). Activity 2.1 will help you to consider and anticipate, or to reflect on different aspects of your first term in teaching.

Activity 2.1

Think about your first term in your first teaching post. What do you think this first term will be like? What are you looking forward to most? What are your worries? Write these thoughts and ideas down. Keep your ideas as we will refer to them again at the end of the chapter.

Follow up: return to these thoughts and ideas after you have been teaching for a term or longer. Did your initial ideas match the reality of your first experiences? In what ways were they the same or different?

What did you think of first? Sometimes the first thing that comes to mind is a feeling of excitement or anticipation; sometimes it is anxiety or even panic. This is quite normal. People generally have a mixture of feelings before starting a new job, especially their first job. If you were looking back to your first term, maybe you had feelings of pleasure – a glow – thinking about things that went well, or maybe the opposite if some things did not go too well. Perhaps one of the first things that came into your mind was a particular scenario, possibly arising out of previous experiences that you have had in the classroom. You may have thought about the class or colleagues you will be working with this year.

The first ideas that come to mind are the hopes and fears that are most crucial to you at the time. This chapter is about acknowledging your hopes and tackling your fears and ensuring that you do not just survive the first term, but you also enjoy it and develop professionally. You may be surprised to find that your hopes and fears are similar to the hopes and fears of a number of the teachers in our study.

For instance, we will see in relation to Abbey, Cathryn, Fatou and Gina, whom we met in Chapter 1, that although they took different routes into teaching, they had many similar feelings and experiences in their first term. For example, they all needed to settle quickly into school life and they also had to establish themselves very rapidly with their new class. It is very likely that you will be able to see yourself in at least some, or perhaps even a great deal, of what they and other new teachers say and describe. What is important is that, as you read about their experiences, you think about how they relate to your own school and class.

Thinking about the first term

When we talked to teachers who were mid-way through their first year of teaching, we asked them to think in particular about their first term and tell us how they found it. What was it like? How did they feel? Was it what they had expected?

The experiences of Abbey, Cathryn, Fatou and Gina illustrate these common issues and concerns very well. When we asked them how they found their first term, all of them said that at some point there were times when they found aspects of their work challenging. This was related to the demands placed on them by the school, the expectations they held of themselves and the amount of time they needed to spend on aspects such as preparation and marking. They all found doing things for the first time difficult to cope with, for instance working with children with specific learning or behavioural needs, or dealing with parents. Although the first term could be challenging, it could also be exciting. For example, when asked about how she found her first term, Gina said:

> Hard but very enjoyable. I was absolutely shattered. People had always said to me that it was hard work, but I didn't actually believe just how hard it was until I was actually teaching.

The first term was challenging and all the NQTs talked about their learning curve and how steep this was, especially in the first few weeks. Like a number of other new teachers, Abbey was learning a lot in a short space of time, but she found it difficult to pace herself. She got very tired and was ill during her first term. Abbey described it as follows:

> Very hard, very very hard. I got very ill; I seemed to get every bug going, every childhood illness. I found I was learning things every day, there's so much to be said for on the job training. It's all the things you've got to get used to, the meetings, the admin, all the little intricacies of school life, the organization and things like that, and really you don't do that sort of thing on your training course, you've got to be in school to do it.

Cathryn on the other hand was tired, but was better at pacing herself and planning ahead. She learnt early on that she could not treat the first term like an extended teaching practice. She also realized that she was now responsible for everything relating to her class, not just the aspects she dealt with on teaching practice. Part of this was because Cathryn looked more holistically at the year and tried to find ways of coping more realistically long-term, as the following quote illustrates:

> Exhausting, the NQT year is so hard, but it's exciting. But I tried to do everything as I did on teaching practice, but you just can't. I'd taken on far more than I needed to. You can't keep going at that pace; you

can't keep writing lesson plans as you did for teaching practice, and being really on top of everything all of the time. There's so much to do, it's just impossible, but no one really prepares you for that, no one tells you how to plan realistically once you're actually teaching day in day out; you've just got to learn how to cut corners yourself.

Fatou was in a different situation from the other three new teachers. She had previously been a teaching assistant and had trained (on the GTP) in the school in which she was now teaching. As we saw in the last chapter, she was very familiar with the school. By the time she reached her first term as an NQT, she had already experienced and overcome many of the challenges which Abbey, Cathryn and Gina were now facing. As we will see in later chapters, Fatou had other challenges to face, but for now, she was looking forward to being responsible for her own class, as she said:

> I really enjoyed it because I had a class all to myself ... On the GTP programme you're basically straight in the class full-time and that's it. But then that wasn't so bad: I knew all of the pupils, I knew their names and I knew all of the staff and I knew the building, I knew how the school worked, I knew their routines, etc. It wasn't like starting fresh, so when I came to my NQT year I was basically working with the same people I'd worked with for years, only now I was a teacher ... I really enjoyed my first term here, I could do whatever I wanted with my class.

We found that the 34 teachers involved in the study raised very similar issues and concerns about their first term. The following three teachers' comments sum up what the teachers said to us:

> I think I found it harder than I expected. I don't think any teaching practice can prepare you for full-time teaching. The professional development you make in that term is just immense.

> Absolutely hell and I never want to go through it again. The first term was just awful. I don't think anything in the world can prepare you for it. Every day you're knackered at the end of school and every day you've got to do more and more. There's always planning and marking to do. I thought that after working every evening and weekend when I was doing the PGCE, things would get easier but they haven't.

> Very hard, but that was to do with the fact that we had Ofsted two weeks after school started, and because I didn't actually know any of the children, I couldn't plan anything until I got into school.

To help you prepare for your first term in teaching, it is important to identify some of the key issues and problems you are likely to face. Activity 2.2 below will help you to do this. Once you are aware of these, you can begin to think of ways to overcome or prevent the problems.

Activity 2.2

Look at the quotes above. What do you think were the main issues and problems facing these teachers and why?

Now think about the issues or problems that you think you will face (or have already faced, if you are looking back). Make a note of these and compare them with those arising from the research.

When we analysed all the data from the interviews with the new teachers, there were four key issues which emerged as important to them. These were:

- Being responsible for your own class;
- Preparation for the first few days and weeks of term;
- Confidence and lack of confidence in the early weeks of teaching;
- Time and use of time.

The rest of this chapter focuses on these issues, reflects more on what they mean to beginning teachers and encourages you to think about how they relate to you as a new teacher.

Being responsible for your own class

One of the most important issues raised by the 34 teachers was being responsible for their own class. They tended to have a mixture of feelings about this. Sometimes they felt excited at the prospect of not being restricted by having to work with another teacher's class. However liberal their mentor had been during their teaching placement, they had still felt an element of constraint. On the other hand, the beginning teachers sometimes felt anxious about being totally responsible for the class. There was no longer another teacher who could take over: there was a realization that the buck now stopped with them.

Abbey highlighted responsibility for her own class as being a really important issue. She explained why she felt like this:

> The main difference is being by myself. I mean, the school does support me, but your class is totally your responsibility. You've sort

of got to be more professional because you are the teacher. I felt more isolated because I had never been in a position where there wasn't someone else who could take over if things went wrong. It wasn't that I wanted someone there, just that I found it difficult knowing that it was me who was fully responsible for my class, and nobody really tells you about that. I know it's obvious, but you don't really think about it until it happens.

She was not alone in thinking this. The comments below reflect the opinions of most of the 34 teachers to whom we spoke:

Suddenly when you're teaching full-time you are in charge and all the decisions have got to be made by you. You've got to juggle everything, but on teaching practice there's always something that you're not responsible for, but then suddenly you're responsible for everything and that's quite different; it's quite a jump that you make from teaching placement to having your own class.

On teaching practice ... you take over but what you do is step into someone else's shoes, and so when you come to take your own class you've got no one's shoes to step into, you've got to do everything from scratch. It was me who had to set up all the organizational systems, and on teaching practice the children know the boundaries of how far they can go with things, but once you start teaching you've got to set those boundaries yourself. You've got nobody's boundaries to take over.

What does it mean to be responsible for your own class? Why do you think so many new teachers highlighted this issue or were often surprised by how unprepared they felt for the first few days/weeks of term? Activity 2.3 below will help you to identify the areas of responsibility you had on your final teaching practice and the associated skills you have acquired.

Activity 2.3

Think back to your final teaching practice during your initial training where you would have largely been responsible for the class, with the support of a class teacher or mentor. Having read what the teachers above said, think hard now about what you were *really* responsible for and where boundaries of responsibility lay (for example, you may have established particular rules for yourself in the class, but your class teacher may have already established the ground rules that had been operating all year).

Activity 2.3 *cont.*

Make two lists as follows (your lists may get quite long):

List 1

List 2

My responsibilities on final teaching practice

What others were responsible for

Now try to identify the skills which you needed in order to carry out these tasks and link these to the national standards for QTS and induction.

Look at the list of responsibilities that you had and skills that you used on your final teaching practice. These skills formed part of your evidence of meeting the standards for QTS (DfES/TTA 2003). Knowing that you can already do these things will help to give you confidence in your new job and will go towards your evidence of meeting the standards for induction (TTA 2003a). However, thinking in advance about the areas for which you were not responsible will give you the opportunity to plan how to tackle these. For example, on your teaching practice you were probably not responsible for establishing ground rules for the class: you would have been expected to work within those already established. One of the ground rules may have been that during class discussions only one person talks at a time and the others are expected to listen. But how was this established initially? This would have been the responsibility of the class teacher but now it will be yours. Being responsible for your class means thinking ahead and being prepared.

Preparation for the first few days and weeks of term

We asked the new teachers what their first few days and weeks had been like. The following comments were typical of the ways in which they described the time:

> I still didn't feel really prepared for those first two days in school and it's not until you're in school that you realize that you're just really not prepared for it, you've still got to learn all about how to handle your class and how to organize them.

> It's a big shock [when you start teaching], it suddenly hits you that you, you've got a class to yourself. I've got reception so that means I'm introducing the children to the school. On teaching placements you're never there when they start, so you never see how the class get to where they are once you actually join it for teaching practice. You

miss out on seeing all of the ways that the teacher shapes the class to the way she wants them.

You've got the class from day one and you've got to do so much with them, and at the same time you're learning more about how the school operates, and who you need to go to for different things and all the little routines you've got to suddenly sort out yourself. Things like when you say to the class 'line up', and they don't know where to line up. It's lots of little things that you just took for granted on teaching practice because the class teacher had already organized them, but when you are the class teacher, you've got all those things to sort out.

When planning for your first days of teaching, there are a number of factors to consider and plan for. Activity 2.4 below and Figure 2.1 will help you to consider in detail the practicalities and responsibilities of the first day of teaching.

Activity 2.4

Take a few minutes to think about the very first day in your first teaching post. What do you think that first day will be like? What are you actually going to do on that day? Be specific: think through the day in detail, from your arrival, right through to the children's departure.

If you are looking back on this day, then try to remember the specific details of what you had to do.

Once you have done this task, look at Figure 2.1 and read through the questions. It is likely that you may not have addressed all of them, because many of these questions relate to routines that would have already been established in your teaching practice class.

Addressing these questions will help you to be prepared for the first few days and weeks of teaching in your new post. Most of you will be teaching in a school in which you have not worked before. You will need to find out about school policies and routines, as well as systems and procedures that operate in the school as a whole and in the year group and/or key stage in which you will be working. Some of you will be teaching in a school you have previously worked in, so you may already be familiar with much of this. As you will remember from your time on teaching practice, being prepared will help to give you confidence.

The first day in school

1   How will the children get to your classroom on that first morning? You may have to collect them from the playground. How will you organize this?

2   How will you make sure that they enter the classroom in a calm manner?

3   How are you going to greet the pupils and introduce yourself?

4   Where will they sit when they come into the room?

5   How will you get to know their names and who is who?

6   Do you know how to take the register and where it will go afterwards?

7   What will you do with the children in that first hour?

8   What about stationery: where will this be and how will you arrange for children to have access to it?

9   How will you organize children moving around the school (e.g. lining up for assembly or going out to play)?

10   How will you greet and introduce yourself to parents?

What else would you add to this list of questions?

Figure 2.1   The first day in school

Confidence in the early weeks of teaching

Many of the teachers to whom we spoke described a swing of emotions in the first term. At times they felt confident, excited, enthusiastic and part of a team within the school. At other times they felt anxious, isolated and worried about their own and their pupils' progress. At these times they frequently felt uneasy about talking things through with others. They told us that often they felt as if they should know the answers and were concerned that others would see their questions as trivial. This happened regardless of how well they were actually doing or how much support their mentor and the others in their school were giving them.

Support and the people who teachers turn to for support are major issues which we will address later. What is important here is that underpinning every beginning teacher's experience or response to events was the issue of confidence. The new teachers often talked about situations that helped to give them confidence. For example, when lessons went well, the teachers got a buzz and felt good about themselves. The following quote from Abbey was typical of the teachers' comments about what tended to give them confidence:

> Today I was doing a science investigation and all the children were really engaged in what they were doing and really enjoying it. It showed in their written work so it's, I suppose it's things like when the children are motivated and when the children say, 'I get it, I understand', that sort of thing, when they really try to grasp a concept that you couldn't get over to them and they get it, that gives me satisfaction.

Remember, you have done really well to have reached this point. Think about all the things you have done well or things that have given you a buzz while you have been training. You need to remember that there will be highs and lows, so hang on to what you do well even when things may not feel as if they are going so well. The following two quotes describe how Fatou and another teacher felt mid-way through their first term.

> Because I trained in an unorthodox way with no exam and no mark, I have never really felt I've been good enough. Although I got through the course fine, with no problems, there's just nothing written down to say that I can do these things. Sometimes when things have gone wrong and I start to question whether I can actually do the job or not, it is good to see my mentor because she really gives me the confidence and tells me that I'm doing okay.
>
> (Fatou)

> I was on a high to begin with, as I'd completed the course and had done well to be offered a place in the school. But by half term I was beginning to doubt myself, I started wondering about whether the class were progressing. I needed someone to say, 'Yes you're doing well'. The head is my mentor and she did observe me and she'd say nice things, but you just sort of wanted someone to come and say, 'That's a good display' or whatever.

You may well find that people you work with will point out when things are not right, and this may undermine your confidence. Don't let it. Often people more readily point out things that are wrong, rather than things that are going well. You may be doing really well and by telling you that something is not right, they may simply be trying to help you. If in doubt seek out your mentor, the headteacher or a trusted colleague and ask them how you are doing. This may help you to keep in perspective the things that you are doing well and help you target any areas you need to work on and improve.

The final issue concerns something which was highlighted by the majority of beginning teachers who took part in our research: time and the use of time.

Time and the use of time

Start by reading the quotes below. Abbey, Cathryn, Fatou and Gina were typical of the NQTs to whom we spoke in terms of their reflections on time and their use of time:

> I rise at 5.30 ... I spend about an hour then checking my files for the day, and maybe doing some preparation. I get to school about 8.00 am and leave about 4.30. Then when I've put my children to bed at 9.00–9.30 pm, I do about another two hours' work. I used to work about five hours a day at the weekends [when I first started teaching] ... the problem is, you never feel you get to the end of it.
>
> (Abbey)

> During my first term I had some real transport difficulties and I had to rely on lifts. I'd be in school by about 7.10 and wouldn't leave until 6.00 or 6.30 and then when I got home I'd do about three hours' work ... I'd try to timetable one day off a week which was normally Saturday, and then on Sunday I'd work from about 10.00 in the morning until 6.00 at night.
>
> (Cathryn)

> I'd be in school by 8.00 and leave about 6.00, but even then I didn't get a lot of chance to do things in school – things like changing displays and marking – so I did (and still do) bring a lot home. So maybe I'd spend one or two hours in the evening working, and then at the weekends sort through all my stuff for the week and then maybe make some games to help in maths or whatever.
>
> (Fatou)

Gina had a young family and preferred to leave school at 4.30 pm and work at home in the evening after the children had gone to bed.

> I'd get in by 8.00 and leave at 4.30, but two days a week we would have one hour meetings after school ... Then one day a week we have a business meeting over lunchtime. Lunchtime is only three-quarters of an hour and these meetings can go on for maybe half an hour, so when that happens, there is barely time to have a cup of tea

before you've got to be ready to start teaching again ... I probably left later [in the day] in the first term. I know how much I work because I worked it out – about 50 hours a week and that includes the one to two hours I do each day at the weekend.

(Gina)

These experiences raise a number of key issues with which you may be familiar. They include:

- Never getting to the end of your workload because there's always something else to do;
- Having no flexibility in relation to the length of the school day and little flexibility over timings of school meetings;
- Having no room for slippage in the day, which means that any outside responsibilities need to fit around school commitments;
- Procedures (e.g. lesson planning and displays) taking a long time and longer than you expect.

We are sure you can add to this list. Anyone taking on a new job will expect to work longer hours and put a lot into it, especially initially. It is exactly the same in teaching. However, if the work is well targeted, putting a lot in usually means you get a lot back. Expect to have to work long hours during the early months of teaching, but you also need to start establishing routines and procedures that will support you and make life easier for you. Try thinking longer term. Activity 2.5 below will help you consider how you use your time and any changes you could make to this.

Activity 2.5

Think about your final teaching practice and the time you devoted to this. Include everything: the travelling, the time in school and the planning, preparation and marking you did out of school. Approximately how much time did you spend on each of these activities each week?

Now think about these aspects in your new teaching post. How long do you spend on each of these activities now? Could you reduce the amount of time spent without reducing the quality of what you do or the impact on children's learning? What could you change to ensure you can realistically get through all aspects of your new workload?

It is likely that you spent long hours each day on the tasks that you have identified. You will not be alone, as most people identify their teaching practice as the most time consuming part of their training. They also identify the school experience as being the most important part of their training. However, as we pointed out earlier in this chapter, your first teaching post should not be treated as an extended teaching practice. Everyone has to learn to make room for both personal and professional aspects of their lives. Abbey, Cathryn, Fatou and Gina, like the other new teachers, expected to have to work hard and for long hours initially, but they also had to learn this balance.

We will return to this issue in later chapters as it proved to be very important. As far as possible, you need to try to avoid being in the same position as the teachers below:

> I do know how long I work now because I've just filled it in on the census. I filled in 60 hours a week because I didn't think anyone would believe me if I put down more, but really I work way over that.

> The thing is, everything I teach I invent because I'm the only Year 3 teacher and there were no plans in place before I got here . . . I've just got to do everything myself.

Key findings and action points

Beginning teachers face a number of key challenges in their first term, including:

- being responsible for your own class;
- preparation for the first few days and weeks of term;
- confidence and lack of confidence in the early weeks of teaching;
- time and use of time.

Being responsible for your own class involves a realization that you have complete responsibility for a class, including setting ground rules for classroom organization and behaviour, within school frameworks. Preparing for the first days and weeks includes thinking through in detail what will be needed to start work on a smooth footing with a new class from the moment the pupils arrive on the first day. For example, how will you get to know their names, relate to parents and arrange the room?

Confidence is something which builds gradually over the first term in teaching, and may grow as a result of children responding positively to some aspect of work in class or positive feedback given by a mentor. It relates closely to support given to new teachers, which is an area we will discuss in more detail in the next chapter.

Time management is a crucial area which often overwhelms new teachers in their first term. Although you can expect to put more time into a new job to start with, it is important to identify ways in which the responsibilities of the work, such as planning, marking or meetings, can be managed alongside a life outside school. This issue needs to be addressed early on if you are not going to experience burn out or get ill from over-work.

Action points

- Identify in advance the issues or problems you think you will face in the early weeks of teaching. This way you will be prepared for them and will have had time to think of appropriate solutions.
- Prepare yourself for the responsibilities you will have to take on as a result of being a class teacher. In particular, prepare yourself for those responsibilities which are new to you, those that you did not have while on your teaching practice.
- Careful planning for your very first day in your first teaching post will help you to establish certain ground rules with your new class. The earlier these rules are established, the easier it will be to establish acceptable behaviour in the classroom and to start to build up a good working relationship with the pupils.
- Have confidence in yourself that you are working well with your class and if necessary seek advice from your mentor or another reliable teaching colleague. If some aspects of your role do not go as well as you had hoped, don't forget to keep this in perspective and re-member you are not expected to be able to do every aspect of your job to a high standard in your first weeks. Think about the aspects of your job that you do well and seek help or advice on those areas in which you are less confident.
- Think about your use of time and try to plan in advance ways of working which will allow you to fit in all of the responsibilities you are likely to take on in your first teaching post. Be realistic about this: time is limited and you need to make time for your personal life as well as your working life.

Concluding discussion

Regardless of age, gender and the support received in school, almost all the newly qualified teachers in our study commented on the huge difference between their experiences during initial training and their experiences of the first term. Many of the problems faced by these beginning teachers arose because of a lack of awareness about what to expect in the first few weeks. Most expected the first term to be like another teaching placement and felt unprepared. Those who coped better had thought through and anticipated some of the potential situations and difficulties that they would face and had prepared in advance for these.

If you look back to the thoughts and ideas that you wrote down under Activity 2.1, many of the issues and concerns are likely to have been addressed in this chapter. We hope that you will also have had an opportunity to consider some aspects of the first term that were not on your list, those unexpected issues that might have come as rather a shock if you had not thought about them in advance.

Starting off in the first term in your new job is an exciting time. Thinking ahead will help to ensure that this is a positive experience. In the next chapter, we will take a longer term view and focus on the first year of teaching. We will consider the experiences of some of the new teachers in our study and will explore different issues raised by them.

3
Looking back over the first year

This chapter draws on the case studies to reflect back over the first year in teaching: the highs and lows, the challenges and the achievements. Using the accounts and experiences of beginning teachers the chapter presents the different ways in which they learn to move beyond survival and begin to develop professional knowledge and skills.

Introduction

As we saw in Chapter 2, by the end of their first term in their new posts, Abbey, Cathryn, Fatou and Gina were coping in different ways with the demands of teaching. They were all working long hours and working hard.

For Abbey and Cathryn, their confidence was increasing, as they were beginning to feel as if they were really doing a good job. However, there were differences. Abbey was very tired and was trying to do too much; she was spending long hours planning individual lessons. Cathryn, on the other hand, was more realistic and was beginning to try to plan longer term. She was trying to pace herself so she didn't overdo things.

Gina was also working long hours, in school from 8.00 in the morning and leaving school at 4.30 in the afternoon. As well as this, she worked at weekends and each evening when her children were in bed. Gina was initially less confident than Abbey and Cathryn; in addition her confidence wasn't growing quite so quickly.

Fatou was in a very different position from the other three at the end of her first term in teaching. She was very confident and had really enjoyed her first term. She had welcomed the opportunity of being responsible for her own class at last. Fatou had completed the GTP in the same school, the same classroom and with the same year group that she was now teaching: she felt confident that she could do anything with her class.

In this chapter we will focus on the whole of the first year in teaching and issues faced by new teachers.

How well teaching practice prepares you for teaching

You are all coming to your first job with a range of different experiences in school. In this section we will think more about how well prepared the teachers in our research felt for their first teaching post. Abbey described it as follows:

> It prepares you as a person and kind of lets you know what to expect, but you really don't find out what it's like until you are actually in there with your own class full-time.

Abbey sums up the feeling of the vast majority of teachers to whom we spoke in relation to the 'jump' from teaching practice to the first teaching post: that is, doing it for real can be very different from being on a teaching practice.

Why is this? At one level the answer is fairly obvious: you're on your own! But that's not the whole story. Cathryn described how teaching practice taught her a lot about behaviour management and classroom management:

> For my teaching practice, I was in a really tough school with huge behavioural problems. I thought I wasn't doing that well ... my mentor could see I was having problems but also that I was dealing with them, and I thought that if I can deal with this sort of thing I can deal with anything. They were really horrible children, but what it did was teach me a lot about behaviour management and classroom organization and that's really where I learned those things.

In some respects Cathryn was lucky to have come across these difficulties when she had a supportive mentor who could help her through it. She was able to learn some really important skills that set the foundations for her career. But more than this, Cathryn was able to establish her own ideas of how to organize the classroom and what behaviour she expected from her pupils and steps she could take to achieve these things. However, she also acknowledged that your teaching practice does not prepare you for all aspects of teaching.

> A lot of what you do on your teaching placements prepares you for teaching, but in some schools you don't have the opportunities to do everything. Like I hadn't been to any parents' evenings ... You're relying on your school where you do your teaching practices to cover these things, and if they don't, well, you just never come across them until you're actually in teaching.

It is really important that you realize that teaching practice cannot prepare you for all the situations that you will encounter in your first year of teaching. Fatou for instance, felt very well prepared for her first year – 'definitely [well prepared], it was like my GTP year was my NQT year' – as she had been a teaching assistant and also completed her GTP in the same school in which she was now teaching. Despite this, she still encountered new experiences; for example, she had not come across some specific additional needs before. Moreover, although she felt well prepared for her first teaching post, her experiences of different teaching contexts had been limited. In the future she may not feel as confident or well prepared for teaching different year groups or for working in different schools.

Have a look at Activity 3.1 below. This will help to determine the aspects of teaching for which your training has prepared you, and those aspects in which you may feel less well prepared.

Activity 3.1

Identify some of the key aspects of teaching in which you feel well prepared and write down as many as you can in 5 minutes.

Now think about any aspects that you feel less confident about, maybe because you have limited experience. Write down the three which you feel are the most important. Now think about how you could address these aspects. You may for instance, be able to approach a member of staff in the school for help. We will return to this issue in the second part of the book.

When you have completed Activity 3.1 you will have two lists. The first list, which comprises those aspects of teaching for which you feel prepared, will give you confidence. The second list, which covers the three areas about which you feel less confident, is also important because it will help you to identify what you will need to tackle yourself or seek help with. Here are some of the areas identified by teachers to whom we talked, in which they felt less well prepared.

> We weren't taught anything about how to take a register, or anything about playground duty, all the things you've got to do once you start teaching; [and] how to hold assemblies, I dread having to do that, I wouldn't have a clue where to start.
>
> (Gina)

> I've got some children with very special needs in my class and I spent the first term getting used to their needs.
>
> (Cathryn)

It's all those little things that the course doesn't actually prepare you for, like the head lice, phoning parents, dealing with notes sent in the morning, that sort of thing. Really all the little things that take a lot of time, and until you're actually the class teacher you don't come across these things, because even on your placement, it's the class teacher who deals with those sort of things.

I'd never had much to do with special needs before and there you are in a class and have a dyslexic [pupil] or whatever, what are you meant to do? There should have been more about dyslexia and things like ADHD and dyspraxia.

[Teaching practice] is a completely different ball game – stepping in, teaching certain lessons and executing lesson plans, with lots of emphasis on subject knowledge and how to transmit it – to teaching a class from 8.45–3.30. Unless you've got children yourself, which I haven't, you don't know what children need. You are their surrogate mother, for 30 children, dealing with issues in their home life, their social life, their emotional needs as well as their educational needs.

Rewards and challenges

Irrespective of how well or under-prepared you feel in the various aspects and subjects of primary teaching, there are numerous rewards and challenges that go with the job.

We asked the 34 new teachers which aspects of their work had been the most rewarding in their first year. This is what Abbey, Cathryn, Fatou and Gina said:

> Well, working with the children is rewarding and seeing them progress, that's just the icing on the cake. It really gives you a lot of job satisfaction to see children progress and you know they are actually learning things that you have taught them.
>
> (Abbey)

> The whole thing, everyday something makes me think this is brilliant, I know why I'm in this job. Even silly things like the child who always asks if they can turn their page over and one day doesn't. 'Yes', you think, it's a breakthrough. Also things like, the staff say, 'Oh that's an excellent display'. It makes me feel really good having supportive staff.
>
> (Cathryn)

Circle time. I felt really privileged to have the opportunity to take the children for circle time and to watch them learn over the year, and how over the year they've also started supporting each other. To see the change in some of the children has been amazing.

(Fatou)

The children, seeing them progress and getting to know them, when children suddenly grasp the concept that you've been trying to teach them, and then it clicks with them. That's the sort of thing I find rewarding.

(Gina)

For all four of the teachers, the children were central to their most rewarding experiences. You may not be surprised to learn that we found that the most frequently cited rewards stemmed from work with the children, their achievements and their progress over the year, as the quotes below illustrate.

Working as part of a team. I feel very privileged to be part of a successful team and also the successes I've had with individual children. The things like when you get report slips back from parents and some parents say, 'Thank you for what you've done,' and it makes you think, yes I've done a lot this year, and by the end of the year the children have learned an awful lot. So it's successes like that that make the job rewarding.

I think that children with the most challenging behaviour who actually have made big changes through the year. Children who I was warned about who have terrible behaviour problems, I've seen how they've improved beyond recognition. That's so rewarding, and also the fact that the children become so fond of you and they really respect you.

All those magic times when someone realizes they can do something, like subtraction, they suddenly realize they can do it, or when the children listen to instructions and really follow them carefully. It is all the little things like that that I find really rewarding.

When the children who I didn't think would get level four actually achieved level four in their SATs, and I knew they'd actually achieved level four because we had all worked so hard at it.

Although the children were often the source of many of the teachers' rewarding experiences in that first year, they also provided many of the challenges cited by the new teachers. For instance, Gina and another teacher said:

> Dealing with the behavioural problems. I've not developed enough strategies to deal with the behavioural problems and I find that really challenging, I know these sort of things build up with time, but I still feel I've got a lot to learn in this area.
>
> (Gina)

> I think what I found the most challenging is actually going through the whole year with the same class, having the responsibility of teaching those children for one complete year.

Sometimes the teachers identified very specific challenges, some of which did not relate directly to the children. For instance Abbey and another teacher said:

> Reports I suppose. They're really awful. I had no life during the time I was writing reports. I'm normally quite organized and I try to get everything finished in school by 6 and then leave it, but for about a month I had no life, I brought reports home every night. I hated the way it impacted on my social life. They may be easier now because I am aware of the formality needed in reports, but last year they were awful.
>
> (Abbey)

> In a sense the teaching assistants because there is so much to think about and so much extra work. You've got to prepare for them as well, and manage them all the time and you have such a close relationship with them in the class, and you've got to be aware that they may be talking about you outside of the class. But you also have to remember that you're the one in authority and in charge and I found that hard to deal with.

These quotes were typical of the kinds of challenges that the teachers we talked to identified. Being responsible for the whole class and what this really meant was something that gradually dawned on the new teachers during their first year of teaching. It wasn't that they didn't know about this or that it was a surprise, but the awareness of the implications became increasingly clear.

Other challenges identified in their first year of teaching were relating to parents, teaching subjects that hadn't been covered in depth during their training, the large amount of paperwork and long-term planning. Many of these areas will be considered in Part 2 of this book.

The next section moves on to look at confidence and the ways in which teachers have developed confidence during their first year of teaching.

Confidence

The rewards of teaching will really give you confidence, as we saw from many of the quotes in the last section. However, at times the challenges you face may diminish that confidence. What is important to remember is that rewards and challenges are interlinked. Overcoming challenges is rewarding but sometimes, until we stand back and reflect, we can focus too much on the challenges and not be aware of what we have achieved. The next two quotes by Fatou and another teacher highlight how pleasantly surprised these teachers were to discover just how much they (and their pupils) had progressed when they reflected on their achievements over the year.

> It was seeing that the children were learning because of what I was teaching them and seeing the children progress. I was actually making a difference to them, but it's not everyday that we do this, we don't congratulate ourselves for what the children have learned. In a way they've taught me more than I've taught them because I know how to teach now and they've given a lot to me. But I think sometimes we need to step back and just see exactly how much we do with the children because we do an awful lot.
>
> (Fatou)

> Getting a view of the progress made over the last year. I didn't realize how much the children had progressed until I got the new intake this year and then I realized just how much work we'd done and how I had brought the children on.

Activity 3.2 below will help you reflect on how far the pupils you teach have progressed.

Activity 3.2

Think about something you have previously taught. This could have been over a short or a longer period of time and may have been something you taught when on teaching practice. For instance, a unit or topic in a specific subject area. Look back at the learning objectives and then focus on one or two pupils. What were you expecting them to learn? What progress did you anticipate them making? Reflect on what the children have learnt and how they have progressed.

<hr />

Activity 3.2 *cont.*

If you are currently teaching the class, you could look at the children's work, talk to them about what they think they have learnt and what progress they feel they have made. You could also look back at what they were able to do in the first week you had them in your class. What can they do now? How much progress have they made?

Follow up activity
A useful task is to track the progress of one or two pupils from start to finish of a work unit or topic. Try to identify what contributed to the progress the children made – it is not always what you think. Talk to the children and ask them what they think too.

<hr />

One very big boost of confidence experienced by many of the teachers during their first year related to them starting to feel like a 'real' teacher, rather than a trainee teacher. What did they mean by saying that they were starting to feel like a 'real' teacher? We will look at this in more detail in the next section.

Becoming a teacher

Becoming a teacher is a long process and when they started in their first teaching post, many of the teachers to whom we spoke said they felt as if they were on an extended teaching practice. Although they were proud and pleased to have achieved qualified teacher status and to be teachers, this didn't mean that they felt like a teacher at all times. Feeling and being a teacher are not always the same. So when did they actually begin to feel like a teacher?

> I certainly didn't feel like a teacher in my first year, I still felt very much like I did when I was a student. I had a difficult class: I mean the staff were supportive but the class wasn't easy. Probably after my first year, when I started my second year I walked into school and knew everyone. I knew the names of the children and thought, 'I taught them last year', and then an NQT walked in and that's when I felt I was a teacher and I was able to share what I'd been through with the NQT.
>
> (Abbey)

> It's something that happens in your first year: you've got your resources together and your teaching starts to come together and you're

in there with them (in the class), and you feel like a teacher. But I suppose the first year is a bit of a nervous year and it's half way through your second year and certainly by the end of your second year you feel far more confident. Like you walk into school to do some photocopying in the morning and the photocopier is broken, and instead of panicking you just think, 'Oh well, what will I do instead?'

(Cathryn)

I felt a fraud for the first few weeks and felt I wasn't capable of doing the job. Maybe 'fraud' is too strong a word, but you know, I didn't feel like a real teacher. But the parents were very very supportive and would come and compliment me. Then one day on a school trip I was sitting next to one of the parents and I let slip that I was an NQT and I said, 'Oh no, you're going to think I'm no good', but she didn't, she said how good she thought I was. So after about six months, because parents kept telling me how grateful they were for what I was doing and kept complimenting me, and because I was observed regularly by my mentor and by the LEA adviser and they told me how well my lessons were [going], it makes you feel like you are doing a good job. I think by being observed regularly, it really helps.

(Gina)

What made them feel like a teacher? In Abbey's case she didn't feel like a teacher until the beginning of her second year, when she was starting the year with a feeling of familiarity, knowing everyone. But even then this wasn't all; it was meeting the new NQT that really did it. She realized that she knew so much more and had something to give to someone who was new. In so doing she realized that she now felt she was a teacher.

For Cathryn, feeling she had become a teacher happened differently. During her first year she began to feel like a teacher when, as she said, her teaching began 'to come together'. What do you think she meant by this? You may have had this feeling on teaching practice when you knew the class and how to work with them; you were confident about what you were teaching and you also had the confidence to know that things were going well. The children were motivated and learning and you knew where you were going with them because you understood how what you taught fitted into the longer term plans. What's important here is that the feeling of things coming together is something which comes from you: you know things are working so you don't need someone to say, 'That's right' or 'Well done' (although obviously that's nice too!).

For Gina, the way the parents viewed her was an important part of the way she saw herself and the confidence she developed. In the quote below, this person was similar to Gina in feeling more like a teacher in their second year. This was because parents and teachers now seemed to see them as a teacher, rather than as an NQT.

> I feel that staff and parents view me as a teacher now and no longer an NQT and that makes me feel a lot better and makes me feel a proper teacher now.

Teachers often began to feel like a 'real' teacher when they were perceived by others as a teacher, but this only happened when they began to develop a teacher persona – but which came first? What the teachers described to us was an interrelationship between the two. So, as they developed as a teacher, they began to be perceived as a teacher and this in turn helped them feel increasingly like a 'real' teacher. This could happen at different stages. Fatou, for instance, began to feel like a teacher during her initial training year, as she explains in the quote below:

> It didn't really happen in my NQT year, it happened when I was training. Before I started I wasn't sure how other teachers and classroom assistants would respond to me after I'd been there as a classroom assistant myself. I just wasn't sure about what their reaction would be like, but it was OK and once I'd realized that people were fine about it, that's when I felt like a 'teacher'. Also, when I met my class for the first time, it was a class I'd worked with as a classroom assistant when they were in reception and one of the boys came up to me and said, 'We know you Miss, because you were our teacher in reception'.

As with Abbey and Gina, this was partly because of the way in which people viewed her, but for Fatou, the timing was more related to the fact that she was doing her GTP in the same school in which she had been a teaching assistant. She wasn't 'new' in the same way in which Abbey, Cathryn and Gina had been. She was familiar with the school routines and the staff and many of the children's names, before she started her training year.

How does this happen? What else helps to make people feel like a 'real' teacher? Again, confidence plays a big part. As we saw above, confidence can come from being aware of your achievements, but it can also stem from other sources. For Gina, the main reason for beginning to feel like a teacher was the confidence she gained from people appreciating what she did. She started the year lacking in confidence and feeling as she said, like 'a fraud', but by the end of the year her confidence had grown as the parents and teachers confirmed to her that she was capable of being a teacher: she was not a fraud in their eyes. Confirmation of your abilities can come from different sources, for example, as Cathryn explained:

We had an Ofsted last term, that went really, really well, and I had lots of positive comments, which was really good.

Another of the teachers to whom we spoke commented on how their confidence had also increased during the first year in teaching. In particular, this teacher felt more confident about organizing the classroom and about meeting with parents, commenting:

I feel far more confident about things like setting up the classroom and organizing the classroom. I also feel far more confident with parents because I'm a familiar face now so I don't really feel like an NQT any more.

But how was this confidence built? In some cases, support from staff in school served to increase teachers' confidence and helped to build and develop new skills, as the two teachers below describe:

I think because I was given so much support from the staff, that gave me confidence. And also we've got some very good staff here, and watching the staff perform and seeing how they teach, that gives me a lot of ideas.

The support from some of the staff. Teachers who have been willing to share good practice and share their successes and failures with you. The camaraderie between me and the staff. They don't want you to feel that you can't cope, they're always there to help you if you have a problem.

Organization of workload

We asked teachers about their workload at the end of their first year of teaching. Many of them felt that, although they had spent long hours on school work during their first term, by the end of their first year, they were able to spend less time on it, while at the same time still feeling prepared for their teaching commitments, as the next example demonstrates:

I'm in a better rhythm now and I don't get so panicked about things, but I am very thorough. I'm trying to be this year, and hopefully being so thorough this year will pay off in future years.

There were still some teachers, however, who at the end of the first year felt that, in order to achieve the level of teaching they wanted, they needed to spend long hours on school work. These teachers felt that they were only just 'surviving' in teaching.

> I think organizing my time and prioritising. I didn't seem to have time for anything. I spent so much time on school work so I've got to learn to organize my time better.

So at the end of their first year, how did Cathryn and Fatou feel? Looking back over the year, in which areas did they feel they had developed most?

> Generally in all of them. I've learned a lot by mistakes, and now it is all starting to kind of come together with all of the subjects. It's just because I've done the full year. I've done all the things you need to do, teach the children, be with the staff, all the organizational things, I've done everything for a year and because of that I've developed as a teacher.
>
> (Fatou)

> Everything. When I now go back and look at things, I realize just how much I've progressed. When I start looking at the subjects I'm going to teach this year and thinking how much my subject knowledge has improved, and how I know different ways to impart information now, that sort of thing.
>
> (Cathryn)

If you've just finished your first year, how do you feel? When did you start to feel like a teacher? In which areas do you feel you have developed most?

Key findings and action points

When we spoke to the new teachers at the end of their first year, they identified a number of issues they faced during their first year of teaching. These included:

- how well teaching practices prepare you for teaching;
- the rewards and challenges of teaching;
- teachers' confidence;
- feeling like a 'real' teacher;
- organizing your workload.

It is likely that your initial teacher training would have prepared you very well for some aspects of teaching and not so well for other aspects. During your first year, and even your first weeks of teaching, you will come across some situations for the first time and may need to seek help with those areas you feel less confident about.

Of the beginning teachers to whom we spoke, the rewarding experiences they had experienced during their first year in teaching related to their experiences with the pupils, in particular to the pupils' achievements and the progress they made during the year. The challenges experienced by beginning teachers also tended to be related to the pupils, in particular to the pupils' behaviour. In addition, beginning teachers also found dealing with reports and parents to be challenging experiences during their first year in teaching, as these were areas in which they had often had little or no experience during their teaching practices. The rewarding experiences served to increase the teachers' confidence, as did overcoming the challenges. Support from the school also played a part in increasing a teacher's confidence. Confidence in turn was one of the factors that helped teachers begin to feel like a 'real' teacher.

The teachers involved in our research also considered that they actually felt that they became a 'real' teacher once they felt a sense of familiarity with the school and those within it. Similarly, when teachers realized how much they now knew, in comparison to how much they knew when they first started teaching, and when they realized that other people, in particular parents, appreciated what they did, this helped them to feel like a 'real' teacher.

Action points

- Identify the areas of teaching in which you feel well prepared, and those areas in which you feel less well prepared. Once these areas have been identified, you can begin to think how you can seek help with aspects of your role which you feel less confident about and those with which you feel less experienced.
- Think about the progress your pupils have made since you started teaching them. The easiest way to do this may be to think about a specific subject area which you have taught and consider the progress individual pupils have made in that area throughout the year. What can they do now that they were not able to before you started teaching them?
- As well as thinking about how much pupils have progressed with their work, consider how much you have progressed in your teaching since you first started teaching, or since your teaching practices. What can you do now that you had difficulty with when you first started teaching?

Concluding discussion

Throughout your first year in teaching, you will come across a variety of situations and challenges for the first time. Even if you have followed the GTP and have taught almost full-time at the school in which you are now teaching as a qualified teacher, there will always be new situations to face, such as coming across a new type of behaviour challenge for the first time or taking on additional responsibilities in school. If you are able to identify the areas you feel less confident about, then you can work out who or what can help you with these and this will serve to help you develop as a teacher.

Your first year in teaching will be a huge learning curve; you will have both rewarding and challenging experiences in the classroom. The rewarding experiences will help to increase your confidence and, if you can learn from the challenges you experience and overcome them, this will help to develop you as a teacher. The point at which you feel you become a 'real' teacher will vary according to your past experience in the classroom, the confidence you have acquired, the way you consider others perceive you and the way you see yourself. If you followed a GTP route, it is likely that you will feel like a 'real' teacher relatively early in your teaching career. Regardless of which initial teacher training route you followed, you will grow in confidence with your work and will gain a sense of satisfaction from looking back and realizing how much you have progressed since you first started teaching. In particular, you will gain satisfaction from looking at the progress made by the pupils you have taught. Knowing that you are largely responsible for their progress is hugely satisfying.

4
Early career development

This chapter concludes the first part of the book by following the case study teachers through their first three years in primary teaching. Even in this early stage, a range of responses and different career paths are beginning to emerge from the wider group, from those who have or are thinking of dropping out, to those who already have curriculum and management responsibility.

Introduction

In Chapter 3, we saw how Abbey, Cathryn, Fatou and Gina were all pleased to have completed their first year in teaching. They had developed confidence in their teaching ability and, when they reflected back on the year, they were all surprised about how much they had actually learnt. Each of the teachers experienced ups and downs throughout the year; however, how they coped during difficult periods varied for a number of reasons.

Abbey and Cathryn received a lot of support from staff in school and this helped to increase their confidence. However, by the end of the first year, Abbey still didn't feel like a 'real' teacher. She felt that she had just survived the year, as she had struggled with a class that she found challenging. She was also spending a long time planning each individual lesson. Cathryn, on the other hand, had more than survived her NQT year: she had had a challenging class during her training and as a result had more ideas about how to work with children with behavioural difficulties. She began to feel like a 'real' teacher during her first year.

Although at the end of her first term Gina was less confident than Abbey and Cathryn, her confidence increased over the year, largely because she was well supported by her school. In addition, positive comments from parents showing their appreciation of her made her feel she was doing a good job. However, Gina was still working very long hours at the end of her first year: she found it difficult to give what she thought she ought to give to both teaching and her family. By the end of her first year, Gina had decided to go part-time.

Unlike the other three teachers, Fatou began to feel like a 'real' teacher during her training. As a result of being familiar with both the school and the age group she was teaching, Fatou made a confident start to her induction year. She built on this firm foundation and continued to develop her teaching skills as the year progressed.

So ... all four of our teachers had survived, or in some cases more than survived, their first year of teaching. But what happened next? How did they get on in their second and third years of teaching? In the next section we will draw together the four teachers' stories, so that you are able to get a full picture of the first years of their careers.

What happened to the four teachers in their first three years?

Abbey

During Abbey's first term in teaching she realized that there were a lot of things she had to learn in terms of subject matter and classroom management, as well as school routines and organizational skills. She worked long hours, she was tired and caught several illnesses during her first term. She felt that she was just managing to cope with the demands of the job. Abbey was 'surviving' teaching but she found her first term very difficult.

Abbey had a difficult class to manage in terms of their behaviour; however, she was given a lot of support from her headteacher and from her mentor. They gave her ideas on how to manage the class and this support helped enormously to increase her confidence in her ability to manage her class.

Now in her first teaching post Abbey realized that, although others in the school supported and helped her, the class was ultimately her responsibility; she was no longer in a position where someone could take over if things weren't going as planned. Partly as a result of this realization, and partly as a result of her having high expectations of herself, Abbey spent long hours preparing for lessons, often getting up early in the morning to check her plans and working late at night and at weekends. As the year progressed, however, Abbey began to realize that she couldn't continue working such long hours. She knew that it was unrealistic to place such high expectations on herself and made a conscious decision to reduce the number of hours she spent on school work. By the end of her first year in teaching, Abbey had moved beyond 'survival' to beginning to work out how she could cope with the demands of teaching, and she was also beginning to have ambitions of becoming a deputy headteacher.

By the time Abbey was in her second year of teaching, her confidence in her ability to teach had increased: she was able to manage her class more

easily and now knew what she expected from the children in terms of behaviour. She was teaching the same year group as she had done in her first
year and found the planning a lot less time-consuming. As she said at the
beginning of her second year: 'The planning's a lot easier, I feel I can put a bit
more imagination into it now, rather than just existing with it'. She was now
coping with the demands of teaching; she felt she was becoming more realistic about school and work and also beginning to be able to balance her
school work with her home life a lot more successfully. Abbey also felt confident about taking on additional responsibilities within school. She became
science coordinator at the beginning of her second year, although she did
point out that she did not find this role too onerous as science had previously
been well coordinated and it did not involve a great deal of additional work.
During her second year in teaching, Abbey also took over the running of the
drama and recorder groups. She was beginning to play a full role in the life of
the school.

Abbey continued to be the science coordinator and to run the drama and
recorder groups throughout her second and third years of teaching. Her
confidence in her ability to teach well continued to grow, as did her ambition
and determination to become a deputy headteacher. During her second year
she commented: 'I will do it, I will make deputy head'.

Cathryn

Cathryn's first teaching post was in a school where she had previously worked
as a teaching assistant. This meant that she was already familiar with the
school building, the staff and many of the school routines. She was also
relatively well prepared for dealing with the behaviour management of her
class. She had learnt a lot on her teaching practice about behaviour management because she had worked with a class that was difficult to manage. As
a result of this she had thought about the behaviour she expected from her
class and how she could work with her class to achieve it. Cathryn was able to
put the skills she had learnt on teaching practice into use once she started
teaching and this proved valuable to her. However, she did have to learn how
to work with children with autism and with Asperger syndrome during her
first year, having had no prior experience of teaching children with these
conditions.

Like Abbey, Cathryn found her first term very tiring: she worked long,
hard days and placed high expectations on herself. However, unlike Abbey,
Cathryn realized early in her first term that she could not treat her full-time,
permanent teaching post as an extended teaching practice. She knew that it
was unrealistic to expect herself to plan in the same detailed way as she had
done during her training. By the end of her first term, Cathryn had made
huge progress in terms of working out a way of managing her time. She had

worked out how she could cope with the demands of teaching in a way that would not allow these demands to take over her home life, while at the same time not allowing the standard of her teaching to fall. She was able to plan with a longer term vision which enabled her to pace herself and her planning. Cathryn was no longer just 'surviving' in teaching: by the end of her first term her confidence had grown; she felt she was doing things well and she was beginning to 'cope' with the demands of teaching.

Throughout her first year, Cathryn was well supported in school by her head and her mentor. Her confidence continued to grow during her first year of teaching, partly as a result of the positive feedback from an Ofsted inspection which took place during the spring term and partly as a result of the positive feedback from staff on how well she was doing. By the end of her first year, Cathryn was confident in her ability to teach well, but she was unsure about whether or not she wanted to take on additional responsibilities in school.

During her second year Cathryn taught the same year group as she had done in her first year of teaching, which made the planning much easier, as she commented: 'I've built up a lot of resources and I've got last year's plans, so I find I'm not doing so much in the evenings now ... I've got one year behind me.'

She was given the role of science coordinator in her second year; however, like Abbey, she did not find this role too demanding as it had been well planned: 'It was just a case of keeping it ticking over'. Cathryn continued to be the school's science coordinator during her second and third years; she also took on the role of design and technology coordinator. Although she had initially been unsure about whether or not she wanted to take on additional responsibilities, Cathryn worked in a small school where all staff were expected to take on additional roles in order to share the workload.

Fatou

Fatou had previously been a teaching assistant at the same school as she was now teaching, which meant she was familiar with the staff, the pupils and the school routines. Her main concern when she first started teaching was how the teaching staff and teaching assistants would view her as she moved from her role as teaching assistant to a trainee teacher and now to a fully qualified teacher, all within the same school. However, these concerns were unfounded, and her transition to teacher was relatively easy.

Fatou was looking forward to being responsible for her own class. During her GTP training she had gained enormous confidence in her ability to teach, as the programme had involved her teaching almost full-time in school during the whole of her training. Unlike Abbey, Cathryn and Gina, Fatou's experience of teaching in the school during her training meant that she had already experienced and learnt how to deal with many of the challenges normally faced by teachers in their first year of teaching. As a result of this, she entered teaching feeling able to cope with the demands placed on her. She enjoyed her first term in teaching and her confidence continued to grow as she was praised by her mentor for the things she did.

Although Fatou still worked long hours and often worked in the evening, she did not feel under undue pressure from this. She found that by the beginning of the second term she was becoming more adventurous with her planning. She was able to draw on the wealth of experience she had gained as a result of working in schools for a number of years, and when planning lessons she was able to apply strategies that she had seen being used by other teachers when she worked with them as a teaching assistant.

By the end of the first year Fatou felt she was managing the demands of teaching really well and, although she worked long hours, she considered that she was able to be very realistic about the professional demands of school and was beginning to balance her school and home life in a satisfactory way. She had taken on joint responsibility for the design and technology coordinator's role and was keen to help with after-school clubs; however, she had no ambition to take on additional responsibilities in school which would take her out of the classroom.

Like Abbey and Cathryn, Fatou taught the same year group during her second year in teaching. She was very well settled into the school by this time and had very few problems coping with the demands of the job. During her second year in teaching, Fatou took full responsibility for coordinating design and technology; she was involved in making a school web page and was helping to run an adult learning club. Like Abbey, she was very much involved in the life of the school.

At the beginning of her third year in teaching, Fatou was asked to teach a different year group. Her training year and her first two years in teaching had involved teaching Year 2 classes and she had become very comfortable with this. She was now being asked to teach the Reception class. She found this transition incredibly difficult, as all of her teaching experience to date had been with the same year group within the same school and she had no experience of teaching in different contexts. In addition, there were particular challenges in moving into early years' teaching of which she had no prior experience. During her first term of teaching the Reception class, Fatou experienced similar anxieties to those faced by Abbey and Cathryn during their very first term in teaching. She spent long hours planning lessons and the demands placed on her quickly impinged on her life outside school. The additional work that was now involved in planning for the Reception class made her feel as though she was just starting out in teaching. She no longer felt that she was able to realistically manage the professional demands on her. Instead, she felt as though she was now just 'surviving' in teaching.

Gina

Gina had spent a large part of her training year away from home as she was unable to find a programme locally where she could complete a PGCE. She was pleased to be back living with her family, but found it difficult to juggle her new teaching career and her family life.

Although Gina enjoyed her first term and was coping well in the classroom, she found the demands of teaching meant that she did not give the time to her family that she would have liked. By the end of her first year in teaching, she was still working long, hard hours and working most nights once her children were in bed. She realized that the amount of time she wanted to spend with her family and the amount of time she was realistically prepared to give to teaching meant that she would be happier teaching on a part-time, rather than a full-time, basis. At the end of her first year Gina came to an arrangement with her school that, during her second year, she would job-share with another member of staff. This seemed an ideal solution as it meant that Gina could continue teaching, as she wanted to, but by working fewer hours she would be able to spend more time with her family. However, during her second year in teaching, as the year progressed, Gina found that she was being asked more and more often to work additional hours at her school; she also found that she was expected to do a lot of the planning for the other job-share teacher, as well as for herself. Gina again found herself in the position where the demands placed on her were more than she felt she was able to cope with if she was to balance her family life and her school life.

Gina resigned from her teaching job at the end of her second year. She then worked as a supply teacher for a year, which meant she could largely work the days and hours she wanted to do. This allowed Gina to spend time with her family, as well as spend time teaching. She was then offered a part-time job in one of the schools where she had worked as a supply teacher. She accepted this post and found the outcome satisfactory. She was working part-time and this school placed very few additional demands upon her, which allowed her to spend time with her family.

So we can see that the four teachers had fairly different experiences during their first three years in teaching. Their aspirations differed and this wasn't always related to how well they felt they were progressing as teachers. In fact, all four teachers had grown in confidence in relation to their ability to manage and teach a class successfully. They had developed professionally over the three years. But how did this happen?

How did the four teachers develop professionally during the first three years?

Abbey found her first term very tiring; she found that there was a lot to learn during her first term and during her first year as a whole. She was pleased that staff at the school had been supportive and allowed her to make mistakes without criticizing her for them. She explained:

> It's such a friendly school, you feel very comfortable here. There were certain things I did wrong and no one actually said, 'Oh you got that wrong.' They just said, 'It doesn't matter, it happens; move on.' They said, 'We all make mistakes.' I think you've got to remember that everyone in teaching is learning. Even after 20 to 30 years, you are still learning, things are always changing. I know you can't reinvent the wheel, but in teaching you've got to be flexible and not afraid to change.

So Abbey found that, by being allowed to make mistakes, she actually learnt from them and this helped her develop further professionally. She also found that learning to deal with parents helped her to develop as a teacher. She commented:

> When you have a really demanding parent on your doorstep de-manding all sorts from you, it actually made me 'hard' and realize that I had to keep a certain distance from parents and I can't be dictated to by parents. So now if a parent asks me to do things for their children, 'Will I do this?' or 'Will I make sure I do that with them, and read such and such with them?' I'm not afraid to say, 'No, I can't do that today, I've got other things planned', and it made me become more confident in what I was doing, because I could actually stand up for myself and say, 'No, I'm not doing that because . . . ' And I think once I learned that, that I was the teacher and I was in charge of what I did, it made me feel in charge.

As Abbey learnt to deal with more demanding parents, she also grew in confidence. She considered that this in turn led to parents treating her as a 'teacher', which also helped to develop her confidence during her first year.

Cathryn felt more prepared for teaching than Abbey. She had experi-enced a class that was difficult to manage during her teaching practice and this had helped her develop professionally and stood her in good stead for her first teaching post. She had also learnt a lot during her first year through working closely with her mentor, as she explained:

With the planning, well, you feed from your mentor, she'd been teaching for years. There were two Year 1 classes and we planned together. She had all the experience and knew what to do and I had all the new exciting ideas so it worked out really well, and of course because I'd worked with children so much before I had ideas from the past.

Although Cathryn had learnt a lot from working with her mentor, she also found that positive feedback from an Ofsted inspection and from other teaching staff had helped to increase her confidence in her ability to teach well. Cathryn considered that the knowledge and ideas she had gained through observing teachers had helped her develop professionally in areas where she was less confident and less able.

I've found the areas I am weak in, like music. I've been able to de-velop those areas by watching others and I've learnt so much from that, it's far better than any course. 'Go out and see others do it,' that's how I'd always learnt things, watching others do it … you never stop learning.

Fatou began her teaching career with confidence; in fact, as a result of her familiarity with the school and the teaching, she was more confident about her role as a teacher than Abbey, Cathryn and Gina. However, as we saw earlier in this chapter, Fatou's confidence fell at the beginning of her third year of teaching when she was asked to teach a year group with which she was not familiar. Fatou had a more limited range of experiences to draw on, as her teaching experience had been relatively restricted.

In my first years of teaching I taught Year 2 classes, but this year I'm teaching Reception and it's like starting again. I wasn't particularly keen on it at first as I realized that there was a lot of work involved. I hated the first term but now it's not so bad, but it's a whole different ball game to teaching Year 2: they just need your time so much and there's so much they have to learn. Also I was meeting parents for the first time and you realize just how different the support at home is. At least when they come to you in Year 2 you have some ideas about their family.

If you'd asked me how I was coping with the demands of teaching last year, I would have said it was easy, as all I had to do was adapt my plans each year to accommodate my class but now, moving to Reception, it's taken over my life. It's a whole different lot of planning I need to do. Also I've got no idea of the children coming up to me, whereas when I had the Year 2 class, I knew the children I would be getting and could plan for them. There's profiles to fill in, just so much to do. It took me 3 weeks of the summer holidays to go through the resources and the first half term I used a different planning sheet every week until I found one that I could use.

Fatou learnt a great deal during her third year in teaching, in particular during the first term of that year. Although she did not enjoy that first term, she developed professionally during the year, as she came across many new experiences for the first time. In some respects with all the new challenges she faced, Fatou's learning curve that year was similar to the learning curve Abbey experienced during her NQT year.

Gina worked full-time during her first year in teaching, but she found it difficult to juggle her family and school life. For this reason, she decided to work on a part-time basis during her second year; however, this still led to some problems:

> I was at my first school full-time for a year because I wanted to get my NQT year finished, but then I wanted to go part-time because it was just too much with a family as well. The school agreed to let me go part-time, but it didn't really work out because I was doing a job share with the deputy head … she was out so much of the time that I ended up being asked to do so much more work, but it wasn't really what I wanted. So then I resigned and I did a year of supply teaching and that was fine. It fitted in really well and some of that time I did supply at the school where my son goes and I said to them, 'If ever a part-time job comes up, let me know'. Then a part-time post did come up and the head asked me if I'd like to work in the school. I'm quite happy where I am but I don't know if I'll stay. I certainly don't want to be a deputy or anything.

During her training, Gina developed in confidence in her ability to manage her class, as her mentor had worked closely with her on this, giving her practical advice.

> She'd tell me things like how to settle the class in first thing in the morning, and talk to me about how she groups certain children together, and about the type of work she gives certain children. She'd also explain the different behavioural strategies she used with different types of children.

Gina's confidence in her ability to manage a class grew during her first year. However, during her second year in teaching (when she was part-time), her confidence fell, as she felt that she was not able to control her class as well as she had done previously.

By the end of my first year I felt really confident with them [the class], but now my confidence seems to have gone out of the window and I'm really questioning myself. If I hadn't have had last year when I could control those children and we got on well, I wouldn't have built up any confidence, but now I just seem to be controlling the children's behaviour rather than teaching. My confidence is really diminishing.

Fortunately, the experiences which Gina came across while she was working as a supply teacher during her third year of teaching, helped to develop her further and she regained her confidence.

Thus, all four teachers developed professionally during their training and during their first three years in teaching, but the ways in which they developed and the reasons for the development were different for each of the teachers. For example, Abbey was allowed to make mistakes during her training and she learnt from these. Then during her first year in teaching she learnt how to deal with demanding parents, which in turn increased her confidence in dealing with parents generally. Cathryn had learnt a lot from having to manage a difficult class during her teaching practice, and during her first year in teaching the support from her mentor, positive feedback from staff and an Ofsted inspection, and the knowledge gained from observing teachers, had helped to develop her professionally. Fatou felt very prepared for teaching as a result of having spent her training year teaching almost full-time in the school in which she was then teaching as a newly qualified teacher. However, her professional development was limited to one school and one year group and when asked to teach a different year group she found it difficult to cope with the demands of this change. Gina, on the other hand, had developed confidence in her ability to manage her class during her training. Her mentor had explained different behavioural strategies and this had served to prepare Gina for managing her class in her induction year. She had then built on this through the range of experiences involved in having to manage the class on her own.

How you develop professionally will depend on the school and the circumstances in which you find yourself. It may be that during your training you do not have the opportunity to deal with a class which is difficult to manage, in which case the first time you experience this may be when you are actually teaching. Your initial teacher training programme cannot prepare you for every aspect of teaching, but by being aware of the aspects in which you have had limited or no experience, you can help to prepare yourself for some of the new experiences you are likely to face.

Activity 4.1 below focuses on the factors which may help you to develop professionally. Remember, it is not just the positive experiences which help you, negative experiences can also help, as we learn just as much and sometimes more from mistakes we have made.

Activity 4.1

Think about the most positive experiences you have had in teaching so far. Which of these have been key learning experiences? What other experiences have you encountered that have helped you develop as a teacher and how did you develop?

Now think about anything that went wrong. Which more negative experiences have you learnt most from? How? What would you do differently if you encountered any of these situations again?

Early pathways in your career

By the time the four teachers had reached their third year in teaching, each had their own ideas relating to where they would like their teaching career to lead them. Some had taken on additional responsibilities such as being the school's science coordinator, while one, Gina, had found the demands of full-time work did not allow her to spend as much time with her family as she wanted, so had changed to teaching on a part-time basis. Abbey was working full-time and had aspirations of becoming a deputy head, while Cathryn and Fatou were very content with their role in school and wanted to remain being a classroom teacher.

Do you recognize any of these experiences? Activity 4.2 below will help you to think about the career path you want to take. Beginning to identify your career path will help you decide the experiences you need to gain in order to fulfil your ambitions.

Activity 4.2

Where are you now in your career? What responsibilities do you currently have? Think about the responsibilities you would like to take on. Do you want to become a subject coordinator like Abbey? Are you currently a subject coordinator but want to take over coordinating a different or an additional subject area?

Now think about where you want to be in five years' time. What skills and experiences do you need in order to achieve this goal? Work out a plan of how you could do this.

Key findings and action points

In this chapter we considered two key issues:

- the professional development of the four case study teachers during their first three years of teaching;
- early pathways in your career.

We have highlighted the professional development of the four teachers involved in the research. A range of factors contributed towards helping these teachers develop professionally. In particular they considered the following factors to have played a significant role in helping their professional development:

- being allowed to make mistakes and learning from them;
- learning from working with their mentor/supportive teacher;
- observing other teachers; and
- receiving positive feedback from parents, Ofsted and other teaching staff.

Not all the four teachers entered teaching at the same level of professional development as each other and, as they progressed through their first three years in teaching, they developed at different rates and in different areas. Abbey, Cathryn and Gina had all found the first year very tiring and at times had difficulty coping with the demands placed upon them. However, by their third year in teaching, they were more realistic about how to manage professional demands. However Fatou, who was initially very confident in comparison to Abbey, Cathryn and Gina, began to lack confidence at the beginning of her third year of teaching when she was asked to teach a class and year group of which she had no previous experience. She was now lacking in confidence and was feeling as though she could barely cope with the demands of teaching.

Action points

- Reflect on your work and think about the improvements you have made in terms of your ability to cope and manage various situations. You will begin to realize how much you have developed professionally since you first started teaching. If you reflect on some of the challenges you have faced and how you have learnt from them, this will also help.
- Begin to plan your career path and think about where you would like your teaching career to lead. If you have aspirations of becoming a subject coordinator or a deputy headteacher or headteacher, then work towards this by developing the skills and experiences needed for these roles. If you share your ambitions with colleagues in school and with your headteacher, they may be able to help you work out how to achieve them.

Concluding discussion

Your professional development will depend on many factors, some of which may largely be out of your control, for example, the level of support you are given in school. However, there is a lot you can do to help you develop professionally during your early years in teaching. You will learn a great deal from working and sharing ideas with others within your school. You can also learn much by reflecting on the work you have done.

This first part of the book has focused on the process of entering teaching, experiences in the first term and first year and, for our case study teachers, a more detailed look at the first three years. Hopefully you have been able to relate to some of the issues raised by the new teachers and have found the suggested activities useful. Above all, what most of the teachers to whom we spoke stressed to us was the huge difference between being on teaching practice and 'doing it for real'. We will finish this part of the book with two quotes which illustrate this.

> It's different having your own class. I'm given lots of support here but it's still my class, and there's no one else in the classroom to take over if there are problems, so you know you've got to get on and deal with everything.

> It's just things like organizing the class, where they sit for the register, organizing them into groups for work ... to a large extent all the little things that needed doing, that you just take for granted on teaching practice.

Further reading and useful website links

Moyles, J. and Robinson, G. (eds) (2002) *Beginning Teaching: Beginning Learning.* London: Open University Press.

Ofsted (2003) *Teachers' Early Professional Development.* E-publication document (on website only). London: HMI 1395, www.ofsted.gov.uk.

Pollard, A. (2002a) *Reflective Teaching. Effective and Evidence-informed Professional Practice.* London: Continuum.

Pollard, A. (2002b) *Readings for Reflective Teaching.* London: Continuum.

PART 2
Key issues and problems: moving beyond survival

Having presented a broad overview of the first three years of teaching in Part 1 of the book, this second part takes a more in-depth approach to the most commonly cited issues and problems identified by the new teachers in our research. Each chapter will consider a particular set of issues and present practical guidance, partly through a focus on how the teachers we spoke to tended to manage the challenges they faced. The main challenges identified by the new teachers were:

- how to deal with the planning and preparation necessary to manage learning in a busy primary classroom;
- how to organize learning experiences and work with pupils with diverse needs now they were *the* class teacher and responsible for all of their pupils; and lastly,
- how to build and handle professional relationships within the school community.

In the first part of this book, we looked closely at the experiences of Abbey, Cathryn, Fatou and Gina and also drew on the voices of a further 30 NQTs. In this second part of the book, we will continue to draw on the experiences and voices of these 34 newly qualified teachers, but we will also draw on findings from our research with two other groups of beginning teachers: a group of 95 new teachers who responded to questionnaires (unlike the 34 mentioned above, these 95 new teachers were not interviewed) and a cohort study of 22 teachers who were all interviewed during their third year of teaching (see Appendix for more details).

The group of 95 new teachers responded to questionnaires sent to all the newly qualified primary teachers in three local education authorities after their first term in teaching and again after their first year. These 95 teachers, together with the 34 whose voices we drew on in Part 1 of the book, made up the total number (129) of new teachers who responded to these questionnaires (a response rate of 48%). The questionnaires included the following areas:

- *General information*: gender, age, qualifications and prior experience.
- *Initial training*: which aspects of their initial teacher training had been particularly helpful/not helpful, and what gaps they could identify.
- *Subject area preparation*: the subject areas, and other aspects of school life, in which they felt well prepared and less well prepared.
- *Subject area development*: the subject areas, and other aspects of school life, in which they considered they had developed most or least.
- *Rewards and challenges*: which aspects of their work had been most rewarding and which most challenging.
- *Areas for development*: their main priorities in the coming year, in relation to their professional development.
- *Futures*: where they saw themselves in five years' time and why.

We draw on these beginning teachers' learning, experiences and voices in this part of the book as we focus more specifically on the key issues and problems that they identified as being particularly challenging in their early careers. It is highly likely that you too will be able to relate to these teachers' experiences.

5
Planning and preparation: getting to grips with the primary curriculum

A considerable amount of primary teachers' time is spent in planning and preparation. This chapter draws on research findings to demonstrate how beginning teachers learn to cope with teaching the range of subjects within the primary curriculum. The chapter also focuses on how teachers cope with other aspects of the curriculum that provide challenges in terms of planning and preparation. Both of these issues are particularly important given the ever changing nature of the curriculum and the number of government initiatives which impact on schools. Practical approaches which teachers have found helpful in getting to grips with the primary curriculum will be presented.

Introduction

In the first part of the book we highlighted the importance of being well prepared and thinking ahead. When you first start out in teaching this can be difficult, as you may not feel confident about planning ahead and you may not know how far forward you can realistically plan. It is likely that your time and energy will be taken up with thinking about the immediacy of the next lesson or the next day rather than planning for the future. A lot of your initial training will have involved learning about lesson planning and enhancing your own subject knowledge. You will take this knowledge with you as you begin your teaching career. Why is it then that a large number of beginning teachers indicate that planning and preparation are among their biggest worries? How do you get to grips with the primary curriculum and all that is involved?

Let's have a look at how three new teachers explained this problem from their own point of view and the ways in which they felt unprepared when they started teaching:

> You're suddenly dealing with the whole school day and the whole child's needs, which you realize is far more than just teaching them, if you are to help them achieve their potential. I really think the biggest weakness [in the training] was just preparing us to teach

subjects, rather than preparing us to cater for the needs of the whole child.

I think there's been a massive emphasis placed on the key areas, that is English, maths and science, and so I felt prepared in those areas, and if you've got a good tutor in the other areas then you're okay, but if you haven't then you just don't feel prepared.

My very first term in teaching, I didn't even know how to take a register! Why weren't we taught that on the course? And all the other things we weren't prepared for. It sounds silly now, but at the time it was really major, things like organizing how to collect dinner money, how to do all these bits of organizing that need to be done.

Can you relate to any of these comments? As you can see, they are all very different and represent just some of the many perspectives of teachers at the start of their careers. What were these three teachers worried about and what can we learn from them? Their concerns arose from:

- Realizing that being a primary teacher is about more than teaching subjects and that there are 30 individuals in the class, all with different needs.
- Knowing that you can never be equally well prepared in all subjects and that there will always be something that you'll find more difficult or have not taught before.
- Becoming aware that there are 101 other things that are part of a teacher's day.

Planning and preparation for primary teaching can seem overwhelming when you take into account everything that's involved, but being aware is half the battle. In this chapter we will be looking at how other new teachers got to grips with the primary curriculum and all it entailed. By the curriculum, we are not just referring to the ten national curriculum subjects and religious education (RE), but also to wider aspects such as cross-curricular links, thinking skills, planning for diverse needs and other important elements. If you are an early years teacher, the curriculum will be that for the foundation stage and you will be focusing on children's development in the six areas of learning, but you will also have to consider other aspects such as the children's social and cultural backgrounds and needs. Whatever the age group you are teaching, there is clearly much to learn in order to plan and prepare for teaching the whole curriculum, not just the subjects.

Prepared to teach?

In Chapter 3, we highlighted that there are some aspects of teaching for which you will feel well prepared after your initial training. However, in your first teaching post it is highly likely that you will encounter situations and experiences which you have not previously come across. This is quite normal and you will find this happens throughout your teaching career as the curriculum changes and as you work with different pupils and colleagues.

As part of our research we were interested in finding out how well prepared new teachers felt in their first term of teaching. One question on the questionnaire which we sent to 129 new teachers was:

> In which subject areas and other aspects of school life do you feel well/less well prepared?

What would your answer have been to that question during your first term in teaching? Now have a look at Table 5.1, which summarizes the main responses from the newly qualified teachers who completed the questionnaires in their first term. How similar was your response to those of the teachers? The top five areas in which they felt well or less well prepared have been included in the table. The numbers relate to the percentages of new teachers who indicated that they felt well/less well prepared in the various areas. As you will see, significantly more teachers felt well prepared in literacy and numeracy than any other subject or aspect of teaching. You will also notice that over a third of the teachers who responded felt less well prepared in the non-core subjects.

Table 5.1 Perceived adequacy of preparation for first term of teaching

Subjects/aspects in which NQTs felt well prepared	% of NQTs who identified this subject/aspect	Subjects/aspects in which NQTs felt less well prepared	% of NQTs who identified this subject/aspect
Literacy	92%	PE/dance	43%
Numeracy	91%	Arts (art, music, drama)	40%
Science and information and communication technology (ICT)	49%	Humanities (history, geography, RE)	39%
Planning	36%	Working with parents	34%
Assessment	35%	Classroom management and SEN	24%

In terms of the primary curriculum the findings were unsurprising, given the strong emphasis on the core subjects within initial teacher training and the primary classroom and the lesser emphasis that had been given to the non-core or foundation subjects. The literacy and numeracy strategies dominated the primary curriculum from the late 1990s, which goes some way to explain why these new teachers felt particularly well prepared in these areas. As government initiatives led to changes of emphasis within the curriculum, for instance with the introduction of the primary strategy in 2003, we found similar shifts in preparedness among new teachers.

Did any of the findings surprise you? One of the things that surprised us was that, in the questionnaires, over a third of the new teachers who responded said they felt well prepared in planning, and yet when we interviewed the teachers later in the year, many of the same ones, unprompted, expressed real concerns about planning. Why was there this difference between what they wrote in the questionnaires in their first term and what they told us when we spoke to them later in the year?

One explanation is the timing of the questionnaire. At the beginning of the year, the new teachers felt well prepared in planning, because they had learnt so much in their training about daily, weekly and medium-term planning, and had planned the lessons and units of work that they had taught on their teaching practices. However, as the year went on, they began to realize how much more was involved in being prepared to teach the whole primary curriculum over the whole year, as opposed to sequences of lessons over a more limited period, and thus in planning for it. As the quotes in the introduction to this chapter illustrate, by the end of the year the new teachers were more aware of the wider aspects of teaching and the longer term responsibilities of a teacher's role, all of which needed to be built into their planning. The more aware they became of what was needed to be planned for, the more concerned they became about their abilities to plan and prepare adequately.

In the rest of this chapter we will go on to look more closely at how these beginning teachers got to grips with the primary curriculum. We will focus on how beginning teachers learn to cope with the range of subjects within the primary curriculum as well as the wider aspects of the curriculum.

Teaching a range of subjects

So, how do primary teachers learn to cope with teaching a broad range of subjects? How do they expand their subject knowledge and repertoire of teaching skills? It is important to become aware of your strengths and your targets for development before being able to think about possible strategies for improvement. We want to stress that, in most cases, we found that the way in which the new teachers to whom we spoke had developed teaching skills and subject knowledge in the areas in which they felt less well prepared was largely through teaching them during their first year. However, in some cases, there were new teachers who still felt as unprepared at the end of the year as they did at the beginning, in particular subject areas. At times it was possible to identify factors which prevented the teachers from making progress; for example, as Abbey and Cathryn explained:

> Well, I'm even more unhappy about music now because music is my subject and I love it ... The only way we get music is if the class teacher can find the time to fit it in. We do have a half-hour sing-along on alternate weeks but that's about it.
>
> (Abbey)

> And with music, someone comes in to teach music so I just don't have the opportunity to teach it, which is great, but it doesn't help me progress in it.
>
> (Cathryn)

You will notice that both these quotes are about music. This was one of the foundation subjects, together with physical education (PE), religious education (RE) and design and technology (DT), in which many new teachers lacked experience and confidence. Abbey and Cathryn were beginning to understand what barriers they faced in relation to teaching music. In Abbey's case it was not subject knowledge, because music was her specialism, but lack of time: the teaching of music was left to the class teachers to fit into their weekly timetable. Abbey found that owing to her having to teach so many other areas of the curriculum music was one of the subjects that tended to get squeezed out. In Cathryn's case, the problem was that someone else was teaching music, which meant as a result that she could not develop her own expertise in teaching the subject.

These weren't the only obstacles they came up against: the new teachers we spoke to identified a number of other reasons why the development of their subject knowledge and/or teaching skills was sometimes limited. Let's have a look at some of the other reasons that Cathryn and two other beginning teachers gave for not progressing in certain subjects:

> Safety in DT, that worries me ... I don't know what children can or can't do at this age, but it worries me about letting them loose with some of the equipment. I think the school as a whole needs help with DT.
>
> (Cathryn)

With music I just hated it, it was my worst subject. I'm not very good at singing so I am using tapes in school, but I'm just not enthusiastic about it and I don't think anything could help me with that. I don't seem to have the energy to cope with music after everything else.

With music and RE. I definitely want to improve on these. I didn't feel as if I did any justice at all to the subjects. The problem is time: I didn't have time to research them properly. There's so much to do, that subjects like music and PE, it's quite difficult to squeeze them in as well.

As you can see from the above quotes, some of the most common barriers to developing subject teaching skills are lack of time, energy and enthusiasm. Other reasons can be lack of support, knowledge and opportunity to teach. Many of the beginning teachers found that during their first year they spent a large amount of time planning for the core subjects. As we saw in Table 5.1, the new teachers whom we contacted were already relatively confident in these areas and had more ideas about the sorts of activities that they could do during lessons. Thus, many new teachers spent time planning for the core subjects at the expense of planning for the non-core subjects in which they felt less confident. Have a go at Activity 5.1 which aims to help you to identify some of the barriers which may be hindering your development.

Activity 5.1

Look back at Activity 3.1. This would have helped you to identify those areas of the curriculum in which you feel least well prepared or least confident. Now try to identify what might prevent or hinder you in developing knowledge or skills in teaching these subjects. Use the examples we've included in this section to help you to decide if the impeding factors are largely personal ones (e.g. lack of enthusiasm or aptitude) or contextual ones (e.g. timetabling issues or lack of school support).

Once these barriers have been identified, the next step is to find ways of overcoming them. Take a few minutes to think about how you might do this. What steps do *you* need to take to help overcome these barriers? What help do you need from *other* people, and how can you ensure you get this help?

So, how did the teachers to whom we spoke work towards overcoming these barriers? In Fatou's case, one factor she identified was a lack of confidence in relation to teaching literacy. She overcame this in the following way:

I worked alongside one of our experienced literacy teachers and I really progressed in that area, so I feel I've really got to grips with literacy.

If confidence is an issue you have identified, working alongside an experienced teacher is one way of overcoming it and developing your confidence. In the next example, the teacher's lack of knowledge in PE had health and safety implications.

At first I refused to teach on the large apparatus until somebody showed me how to do it. I thought that from a health and safety point of view it was just too dangerous for me to teach PE, so I used my non-contact time to watch other people teach on the apparatus and teach other aspects of gym and games. The teacher who takes my class during my non-contact time was happy for me to do that, and she is really a good teacher, so it was hugely beneficial for me to watch her.

As with Fatou, this teacher drew on the help of an experienced colleague. A slight difference, however, was that rather than working alongside another teacher, they were able to use their non-contact time to observe the teacher, and this helped to develop ideas about how to teach PE. Abbey felt she lacked subject knowledge and teaching experience in relation to ICT. She was lucky, from the point of view that a number of other teachers in the school felt the same way and the school organized some training in this subject area.

New teachers drew on a whole range of strategies to help them fill their gaps in subject knowledge and/or teaching experience. These included learning from the expertise of more experienced teachers and making the most of the opportunities in school; for example, in Abbey's case she was able to take advantage of ICT school-based training. Don't overlook the chances you may get to go on external courses too, and don't forget that the most important resource is yourself. In some cases you may need to rely on your own initiative to find ways to overcome barriers. This might be through personal research, using the internet, school and library resources, or talking to and observing other teachers. In each of the examples given in this section the teachers first identified the factors that were delaying or preventing them from making progress.

It is difficult to tackle everything in one go, so it's perhaps helpful at this point to consider some general strategies that new teachers used when developing their teaching skills in a broad range of subjects. First, focus on your areas of strength; this will enable you to feel more confident generally in your teaching. Second, identify the subject areas in which you feel less well prepared and try to ensure that you have the opportunity to teach these subjects.

In most cases, you will find you develop strengths in these subject areas through simply having the experience of teaching them. Finally, it is important that you take time to think about your experiences and identify any factors impeding your progress.

Planning for the whole curriculum

As well as the specific challenges presented by getting to grips with some still relatively unfamiliar subjects, many new teachers grappled with planning for the whole curriculum. Earlier in the chapter, we looked at the shift in new teachers' attitudes to planning, from feeling well prepared when they started their induction year to a gradual realization that there was much more involved in planning than they had anticipated. Planning emerged as a major concern for them later in the first year of teaching. Let's look in a bit more detail at the reasons for these concerns, starting with one new teacher who explained what was included in daily planning:

> [I do] detailed plans for each day, that is for literacy, numeracy and two other subjects each day, with all the learning objectives and a very detailed outline of what we'll be doing, our learning intentions, questions we'll be asking, the teaching activity and individual and group activities for all groups.

This kind of detailed individual lesson planning was familiar to the beginning teachers, because this is what was expected when they planned lessons that they taught on teaching practices, and most new teachers felt confident about this. However, the same NQT went on to say:

> It takes me hours to plan now, it used to take me two hours, it takes at least six now ... for the LSAs [Learning support assistant] we need to write out a separate sheet with the learning intentions and what that individual LSA will be doing with a group of children and we need separate ones for each LSA.

In this case, one of the reasons why planning took a lot longer than before was because it now had to include detailed, separate plans for the learning support assistants (LSAs), an aspect that this new teacher had not had to take into account before, so daily lesson planning was already being extended to include working with other adults in the classroom.

As well as the increase in what needed to be included in daily planning, another new teacher talked about the other levels of planning that were now required:

> We do weekly literacy plans, weekly numeracy plans and weekly plans for everything else altogether. In these plans we write down our targets and objectives and the activities we're going to do, and the head expects them to be in on a Monday morning ... With our medium-term plans, we do one for maths, one for English and then one lot of medium-term plans for all the other subjects.

Although beginning teachers would have covered weekly and medium-term planning in their training, and would have had some experience in doing it during teaching placements, they were now fully responsible for this, not just for literacy and numeracy, but for the whole curriculum. Many NQTs would have used the school's existing medium-term plans for their teaching practices, but now they had to do these for themselves. The number of different levels of planning and the extent of the planning required 'for everything else altogether' thus led to them often feeling overwhelmed.

From the planning point of view, as well as the children's needs, they now had to consider organizational issues such as grouping, target setting and progression towards objectives through the different levels of planning. Many NQTs only began to realize the depth and complexity of planning and what it actually involved as the year went on, particularly in terms of issues of progression and continuity.

For many new teachers, the real purpose of planning sometimes got confused with demands for accountability, such as how much planning was required for checking by the headteacher. For example, part of the pressure on the beginning teacher in the earlier quote, was that the head expected to see each teacher's plans every week. In the next example, the NQT also described the amount of planning and replanning that was done:

> It's crazy the amount of paperwork: we write our long-term plans as a team and then our other plans we write in rough and then again in neat and then we write our daily plans. It seems crazy to repeat all this work. I know the school has to cover itself and have everything in place for Ofsted and things, but there must be a better way to do things than all this repetition of work.

What is evident from the above quote is that planning was not being required just in order to teach lessons, but to satisfy internal or external demands, such as the headteacher or bodies such as Ofsted. The new teacher acknowledged that schools had to be accountable, but questioned the amount of what was seen as pointless repetition. Planning in itself was getting lost in the more generic term 'paperwork'.

Concerns about the amount of paperwork were very frequently expressed by new teachers who often talked about paperwork as though it was something completely separate from teaching itself. But to what were they actually referring? Well, most of their statements related back to planning, and the amount of planning that was required, but the paperwork aspect was perceived as being on top of everything else, not an integral part of their job, as in the next example:

> You want to do everything you can with the children, and make the classroom a challenging environment, then on top of all that, you've got to do so much paperwork.

What these teachers were experiencing was the seemingly 'endless' amount of paperwork, which they saw as being on top of other demands on their time and separate from the central job of teaching the children. They were also concerned about 'at the end of the day not being able to leave it all behind'. As well as planning, NQTs talked about the amount of work required in record keeping and report writing, both important for internal and external accountability. Excessive paperwork and other administrative demands on teachers have been recognized as forming a large part of teacher stress. One of the key aims of workforce remodelling is to reduce unnecessary paperwork, transfer some duties external to teaching to administrative staff and give teachers dedicated non-contact time for planning. This should go a long way to reducing this particular aspect of pressure on new teachers.

However, even if teachers are allocated some non-contact time because of the breadth of the curriculum, there is still a great deal of planning involved in primary teaching. So how can new teachers keep on top of it? Well, personal organization and time management are crucial. Another way is to work together with other teachers in order to minimize what each individual has to do. Earlier in the chapter, we saw several examples of beginning teachers working alongside other teachers to learn more about particular subjects, and this is a good way to help with planning too:

> I do my planning with a very experienced teacher. The school has put me with a Year 4 teacher who has 20 years' experience and they have given me the easier Year 4 class and she's got the more difficult one, so we plan together and she's been such a good help.

> I do lesson plans with the Year 5 team; we've a three form entry and we all work together on those. We do our weekly plans in our folder; we don't actually give them to the head, but I'm sure he keeps an eye on things and knows what's going on. We have a very good structure for our planning.

Not all schools demand the same level of paperwork and planning, and this can make a crucial difference to whether new teachers feel that they are on top of the job or not. The attitude of the headteacher is paramount in the amount of planning required, as we can see in the second example above and in the following quotes:

> The head is very relaxed about paperwork ... I do long- and medium-term plans for literacy, numeracy and one for the foundation subjects. I do the evaluations and assessments as I go along. I just do what I do basically.

> He [the head] doesn't expect individual lesson plans: we write a weekly overview in reasonable detail so that we can teach from it and we hand it in to the head on a Monday morning ... The school really has gone to great lengths to try and bring the paperwork down to a minimum.

A certain amount of planning that has to be checked by the headteacher can be perceived as helpful to a beginning teacher, as in the next example:

> The head sees my weekly plans and it boosts my confidence writing them, because I feel well planned.

Looking at all the above examples, there are obvious differences between the schools and the headteachers in terms of the amount and level of planning required, but there are also differences in the beginning teachers' attitudes to this. Some teachers felt completely overwhelmed by the amount of planning they had to do, and this was enough in some cases for them to question whether they wanted to stay in teaching. Some found the process of planning with other teachers, or even giving their plans to the headteacher, a useful part of their own professional development and learning. So, as with other aspects of a teacher's work, the way you approach it and respond to demands is important as it can affect whether or not you make the most of the experiences that you are facing.

Key findings and action points

In this chapter, we looked at:

- general preparedness;
- planning to teach a range of subjects;
- planning for the whole curriculum.

New teachers tended to start confidently and were happy to teach the core subjects (especially literacy and numeracy). Throughout their first year, they made progress by increasing their subject knowledge in these core areas, as well as gaining new ideas on how to teach them. However, they tended to start feeling less well prepared for the non-core subjects, and then not to develop so fast, often due to circumstances beyond their control. Ways in which they developed confidence in these non-core areas included observing and working alongside experienced teachers, using school resources and drawing on their own ideas and initiative.

In terms of planning and paperwork, we saw that schools differed greatly in terms of how much was required, and this could affect to what extent new teachers felt on top of planning or not. Planning with other teachers was very helpful, as was the attitude of headteachers who required less detailed or less frequent planning.

Remember the following action points if you are feeling that all the planning is getting too much or that you may never feel confident in certain subjects.

Action points

- Use the whole school context to your advantage: the school strengths, the staff, the policies, etc.
- Help yourself: don't just avoid subjects you don't feel confident about, find out things, make resources, use the internet, etc.
- Attend courses within or outside school which you consider will increase your confidence and skills in areas where you feel less well prepared or experienced.
- Pace yourself and stay well organized, making the best use of your time and energy.
- Observe experienced teachers: work alongside them and ask them to watch you or go through your plans.

Concluding discussion

Let's finish this chapter by thinking about two issues which stand out in this chapter. First, much depends on the school context in which you are working and the type of leadership within it. This can make a considerable difference to what you are expected to do in terms of planning and the level of accountability that is required. However, second, even in the same context teachers respond differently, so a great deal is down to you and the way you respond to the environment you are in. This is where personal initiative and enterprise come in. We saw several examples of new teachers who had identified contextual or personal barriers to their development and then overcome them by making the most of the resources, opportunities and experience of other teachers to help them. Remember this when in the next chapter we look at some of the teaching and learning issues that you will face as a new primary teacher.

Further reading and useful website links

Dean, J. (2004) *The Effective Primary School Classroom*. London: RoutledgeFalmer.

Gipps, C., Hargreaves, E. and McCallum, B. (2002) *What Makes a Good Primary School Teacher?* London: RoutledgeFalmer.

Hoodless, P., Bermingham, S., McCreery, E. and Bowen, P. (2003) *Teaching Humanities in Primary Schools*. Exeter: Learning Matters.

Penny, S., Young, S., Ford, R. and Price, L. (2002) *Teaching Arts in Primary Schools*. Exeter: Learning Matters.

Wood, E. and Attfield, J. (2005) *Play, Learning and the Early Childhood Curriculum*. London: Paul Chapman.

A useful resource is also the government's standards website at:
www.standards .dfes.gov.uk

6
Teaching and learning: working with pupils

Working with pupils in the classroom is a central part of the primary teacher's role and this is the focus of Chapter 6. Some of the aspects that beginning teachers find particularly difficult are dealing with the range of abilities and needs of the pupils and the challenge of behaviour management. In addition, the current emphasis on assessment, testing and accountability places a particular burden on all primary teachers, but especially those in their first years of teaching. Taking the same approach as in the previous chapter, positive and practical strategies will be considered in the light of individual teachers' experiences.

Introduction

Underlying the National Curriculum is the principle of entitlement: that every child should have the opportunity to achieve his or her potential as far as possible. This principle also underlies inclusive schools and the recent government initiative *Every Child Matters* (DfES 2004a). For primary teachers, this can present challenges in terms of teaching and learning, particularly for those of you who are just starting out in teaching and who are working to address and meet the diverse needs of all the children in your class. Differentiated teaching, supporting and extending the least and most able pupils, and above all, setting high expectations and standards for all, irrespective of gender, ethnicity, race, disability or social background, are all part of the day to day role of a primary teacher. It is not surprising that beginning teachers can feel overwhelmed at times. In this chapter, we will look at some of these vital aspects of the primary teacher's role and help you to identify and understand some of the key issues that you may face as you meet these challenges.

The inclusive classroom

Out of all the above aspects of an inclusive classroom, one of the biggest challenges identified by the beginning teachers to whom we spoke was dealing with the range of abilities and needs they found in their class. For example, at the beginning of her second year, Cathryn commented:

> Last year, I had one autistic child, one traveller boy and a boy with Downs Syndrome, and if I'd known a bit more about them at college I might have known how to handle them better. [Now] I've got two autistic children and one with asperger ... so I have had to learn so much about them.

Cathryn's first reaction was to look back at her initial training and wish there had been more coverage of, for example, special educational needs (SEN). However, she also realized that there was a great deal to learn about the different needs of the individual children in her class and that it would not have been possible to cover all of this during her initial training. Another teacher we talked to made this point about the wide range of needs that teachers may encounter:

> We had lots of lectures on special needs on the course but it still didn't seem to cover everything. I don't really know what you can do because every special needs child is different. We did have a fairly good input on the course, I suppose. We were taught about IEPs [individual education plans] and targets, and different kinds of special needs. I just think maybe it's one of those things that you have got to learn on the job.

This new teacher came to the conclusion that there was a limit to the areas that initial training could cover, and that this was an aspect of their role that they would have to learn by experience. The teacher also stressed that, regardless of the aspects covered in training, every child had different needs that would have to be individually identified and met.

Several teachers mentioned that one of their biggest challenges was teaching children with more severe special needs, as in the example below.

> I've got one statemented child in the class and I've got one child who had been to a special hospital school and it was recommended that he didn't go into mainstream school, but basically there's nowhere else for him to go so he was with us throughout the full year. He's gone now but it was really difficult teaching him. I had three special needs children altogether which isn't a lot, but with one as severe as

this child was, it made it very difficult, and also I didn't even have full-time help with him.

In this case, the lack of support together with uncertainty surrounding whether or not the child would stay in the school, were problematic for the beginning teacher.

Before we turn to possible solutions or practical strategies that you can use, let's return to the point made earlier about every child's needs being different and think about this in relation to your own experience up to now. You'll notice that the examples referred to so far focus mainly on children with learning difficulties, behavioural problems or disabilities, although Cathryn also mentions traveller children. We found that, among the new teachers to whom we spoke, quite a common reaction to having a diverse range of children in the same class was a tendency to label some children, albeit unintentionally, as 'problems', thus casting the children themselves in a negative and problematic light. However, rather than seeing the child as the problem, we need to focus on the barriers to learning which exist and on how to overcome these barriers within the classroom.

Now try Activity 6.1. This activity focuses on diversity in the classroom and helps you think about this in relation to your teaching.

Activity 6.1

Think about the children in your current class or a class that you taught previously. How diverse are/were the needs of the pupils within the class?

Now focus on two pupils with differing needs. What barriers to learning do they experience? How have you addressed these so far in your planning? Think about how you have provided for the pupils' academic, as well as their social and emotional needs. What challenges did you need to overcome in order to ensure their needs were met? What steps have you taken to build relationships with each of these pupils?

Hopefully you will now have had time to reflect on the diversity of your class, how you are beginning to provide for identified needs and what other sources of support there may be in school. You may also be clearer about who you tend to focus on; for instance, depending on your class, is it those with special educational needs, the traveller children, or pupils with English as an additional language (EAL) that you tend to focus on first? Or, perhaps is it always the 'naughty boys' that you think about first? Are you sure it is always the 'boys' who are the 'naughty' ones?

When you start teaching, it tends to be the aspects in which you feel least prepared that present you with the biggest challenge, even though they may not be problematic in themselves. You need to be aware or become aware of your own biases and preconceptions and try not to label children because of your attitudes, otherwise you may well find yourself with a self-fulfilling prophecy (e.g. the 'naughty boys'). Let's think about EAL, for example: some new teachers lacked confidence in this area because of limited previous experience. In contrast with most of the new teachers to whom we talked, Abbey was teaching in a multi-ethnic school, which she described as follows:

> We have lots of migrant children in our school ... We teach so much English as a second language to children here and that was all new to me, but because we have so many I've got to do it and we get a lot of support here. So I really feel I've developed within that area.

Instead of perceiving this as a problem, this was something which Abbey had to address on a daily basis, so although she lacked experience to begin with, she soon learnt how to teach the EAL children alongside the others. One important factor was that the school context was supportive and there was expertise within the staff who were then able to help Abbey's own professional development in this area. Many of you will be teaching in schools where there is a range of first languages among the pupils. As with Abbey, you could draw on the experience of the teachers and support staff to help you. Through their experience of working with these pupils, they can offer advice on appropriate teaching and learning strategies to use.

Another beginning teacher's main challenge was related to the gender mix within their class:

> Last year I had some particularly problematic children: they really rubbed each other up the wrong way. I had 21 boys and a lot of them just lacked enthusiasm so I found that really difficult.

Owing to the large number of boys in her class, this teacher started to see boys as synonymous with problems. Teachers can often express this kind of view even when the number of boys is less than this, since boys' behaviour is often reported as difficult to deal with. In this case, the boys' behaviour may have been related to their lack of enthusiasm and we need to question why this is rather than focus solely on problematic behaviour. However, another way of looking at this situation would be to ask, how is this teacher going to meet the needs of the minority of girls in the class?

When asked about which areas teachers felt well prepared or less well prepared, none of the teachers in our survey mentioned gifted and talented children, although all schools are now required to have a policy on this area and to think about how to address the needs of the most able children. We don't know why this group of children were rarely mentioned by beginning teachers, but it is possibly because these children were not so immediately evident as others, and were not perceived as causing problems on a daily basis. However, it may be that some of the children who presented challenging behaviour were actually of high ability but their needs were not being met within the school. Just as the teacher above might be overlooking the needs of the girls in her class, new teachers may be forgetting the potential needs of a small number of gifted and talented children.

As a primary teacher, you can expect there to be a diverse range of pupils in your class. On teaching practice your class teacher may have taken responsibility for some individual pupils so this may be the first time you are responsible for meeting the needs of the whole class, both in the short-term, on a day to day basis, as well as in the longer term. In the first instance in order to work successfully with all pupils, in particular those with additional needs that you may not have encountered before, you may find it helpful to draw on the expertise of others. For instance, one source of support which several new teachers mentioned as being particularly valuable was working closely with teaching assistants who are often very experienced at working with particular pupils or groups of pupils, for instance, children with autism or dyslexia, or pupils with specific physical or emotional needs. They may also have undergone training in a specific area. Don't be afraid to ask their advice and make the most of their expertise in different areas. Their advice can be invaluable in helping you to learn how to enable these children to achieve their potential. We'll be looking at working with teaching assistants more fully in the next chapter, but at this stage start thinking about how you could work with the teaching assistants in your class to help with individual children or groups of children. If you have a teaching assistant allocated to your class, either on a full-time or part-time basis, you will need to start planning ahead in order to make the most of their expertise.

Another source of experience and support is the school's special educational needs coordinator (SENCO) or, depending on the school you are in, there may be language specialists or minority ethnic support teachers. Find out who these teachers or support staff are as soon as you can when you start working in a school, or even before term starts if you have the opportunity to do this. Talk to them about the school's policies on inclusion, as well as the teaching resources available to help groups and individual children in your class. They will be able to suggest a range of teaching strategies that you can try and will also have a lot of useful information about individual children in the school and how to adapt your teaching to ensure you meet their needs. You may find yourself in a school with a special unit, for example, for speech and language difficulties or hearing-impaired children. This will give you instant access to specialist support and expertise.

In addition, find out about the range of visiting specialists, such as speech therapists, educational psychologists, language experts and minority ethnic advisory teachers, who can all play an important role, both diagnostically and in terms of practical support. They may work with children on a one to one basis during their visits, but can also give advice about resources and approaches to use in the classroom. With the *Every Child Matters* (DfES 2004a) agenda, there is an increasing focus on multi- and interagency work. This is a significant development which places the child at the centre of professional working and extends earlier concepts of the ways in which agencies have previously worked together. Have a look at some of the websites and other references at the end of the chapter, as there are a lot of easily accessible teaching materials and information available to help you. Remember that you aren't expected to know everything yourself, but you are expected to work with others to ensure you meet the needs of all the children in your class.

Above all, focus on the way in which a diverse range of pupils in your class can enrich your work as a teacher as well as enrich the learning experiences of all the children.

Behaviour management

Our research also highlighted that one of the areas which beginning teachers often find particularly challenging is that of behaviour management. If you are not in control of classroom behaviour, then very little learning is going to take place, so it is not surprising that this looms large among new teachers' concerns. The term 'behaviour management' can mean a range of things, from controlling a class to managing individual challenging children, and it is almost impossible to prepare teachers during their training programmes for all the behavioural issues they are likely to encounter during their early months in teaching.

When asked what they considered to be the most challenging part of their work, one of the teachers we spoke to commented: 'some really difficult children behaviour-wise ... children who constantly chatter, and children who always draw attention to themselves, but in a negative way'. Another new teacher described problems with:

> Angry children and children I don't know what to do with because of their bad behaviour. But angry children, especially little ones like I teach, I didn't know how to handle it and I still don't to a large extent, but I think I'm getting there.

These comments illustrate some of the concerns experienced by beginning teachers from low-level disruption such as chattering to specific aspects of behaviour management. Some, such as the teacher below, were of the opinion that their training programme did not include a sufficiently large input on how to deal with behavioural problems.

Children's behaviour ... trying to control them I've found quite difficult. I think we should have done more work on behavioural management during our training course.

Other teachers, however, acknowledged that even if initial training covered behaviour management in detail, it would not be possible to cover all aspects of behaviour that teachers were likely to come across, as every class is different. Abbey, for example, considered that the way you deal with many of the behavioural issues you encounter was as a result of actually being faced with them in the classroom and then working out for yourself how to deal with them. As she explained:

Although we talked about behaviour management at university, it was very theoretical. You really have to experience it ... it's down to experience. You've got to experience some kinds of behaviour to learn how to deal with it.

When learning how to deal with behavioural issues, it is important that you are confident with the strategies you decide to use and that they fit into the way you teach. Several teachers, such as Abbey, considered that they learnt a lot about behaviour management only as a result of experiencing different behavioural problems and then devising their own coping strategies. But if your experience has been more limited, you may not have had the opportunity to develop such strategies. As Gina pointed out: 'I've not yet developed enough structures to deal with behavioural problems and I find that really challenging.' Gina was just beginning to acquire some behaviour management strategies to deal with the situations she was now encountering in the classroom.

As well as learning from experience, and increasing their repertoire of strategies, some teachers were also able to pick up ideas through observing other teachers and seeing what strategies they used. Having observed other teachers, they were then able to incorporate some of these behaviour management strategies into their own teaching. As Cathryn pointed out:

I've come across all sorts of problems I hadn't come across in teaching practices, behavioural problems, that sort of thing, and I've just picked up tips from observing other teachers and through my own experience.

We will see how important it is to learn from experienced teachers more fully in Chapter 7.

It may be that your main concern relating to behavioural management involves only one or two pupils in your class whose behaviour you find particularly difficult to manage. It may be, on the other hand, that you are experiencing problems generally with managing the behaviour of the whole class. Whichever is the case, if you are experiencing behaviour management problems, you may find Activity 6.2 below helpful.

Activity 6.2

Think about your current class or one you taught previously and the aspects of behaviour you find/found particularly difficult to manage. Then, taking each aspect of behaviour in turn, try to identify what it is about the behaviour that you find challenging. For instance like the teacher earlier in the chapter you may have found constant chattering difficult to stop.

Now make a note of the ways that you have tried to deal with the various aspects of behaviour that you identified above. Which strategies were more successful? Why do you think this was? How do other teachers deal with these issues? Could you incorporate any of their strategies into your practice?

Once you have identified which strategies work for you and why, as well as which aspects of behaviour management you find challenging and why, then you can begin to think about what to do. Here are some suggestions:

- The first thing to be clear about is the aspect of behaviour which you are finding problematic, e.g. children chattering in class.
- Once you have decided on this aspect, you then need to focus on a specific context or situation in which it occurs, for instance children chattering at the beginning of the lesson when you are trying to address the whole class. You may need, for now, to ignore other contexts or situations in which children chatter.
- Think about the strategies you have already tried, then think about to what degree they have worked and with which pupils. For instance, you may have tried waiting for silence but found that this took a long time. Or, you may have asked the class to stop chattering but may have had to do this several times before you achieved the result you wanted with certain pupils.
- If you feel the strategies you use aren't proving sufficiently successful, a member of staff could observe you to help determine how the class is responding. In discussion afterwards, you may be able to identify how to adapt the strategies or adopt new ones. Alternatively you could observe another member of staff with a view to learning from them about their behaviour management techniques.

There are a number of helpful books on aspects of behaviour management, some suggestions are given at the end of this chapter.

Assessing children

In the last chapter, we looked at the demands of planning and the challenges this presented to new teachers. Just as good planning is essential to teaching, so is the assessment of children's learning. However, this was an area identified by beginning teachers in which they felt they had relatively little experience and lacked confidence. Some of the new teachers to whom we spoke said that, although assessment was covered in detail during their training programme, this was more from a theoretical point of view than from a practical perspective. As one of the teachers pointed out:

> We spent a lot of time learning about assessment, but the course was so focused on you understanding what assessment was and understanding different types of assessment, and on the tutors assessing you, that there wasn't much time spent on telling you how to apply the assessment procedures within school.

Abbey voiced her concerns vividly:

> As far as levelling goes, at first I hadn't a clue, I had only ever levelled one piece of work and that was for an assessment. I used to dread being in the staffroom when people were talking about levelling because people would say to me, 'Well, so and so is a level two or a level three,' and I'd think, how do they know what they are? I just didn't understand it, I just didn't understand how they knew. I am getting more used to it now.

Abbey was expressing worries about a specific aspect of assessment: levelling. Trainee teachers are not expected to be able to level without help from an experienced teacher, even by the end of their initial training. Abbey, along with some of the other teachers to whom we spoke, found levelling difficult to begin with. It may be that you are experiencing the same sort of anxieties over levelling or other aspects of assessment: either you do not feel fully prepared by your training programme or you do not feel able to put what you have learnt into practice. These concerns are very common and it will take time to build up confidence in how to assess the children you teach.

The school you are currently working in, or where you are intending to work in the near future, should have an assessment policy. You will need to adhere to this, however within the boundaries of what the school assessment policy expects from you, it is important that you develop approaches that you find easy to use and that are not too time-consuming. As with planning, the amount of assessment that new teachers are required to do can vary from school to school. A lot depends on the school policy and the requirements from senior staff, as this beginning teacher stressed:

> I do find the assessment hard but that's not because of the head, it is because of our assessment coordinator. We assess each child in English each term; for example, we may do a writing assessment and level each child's writing. In science we level and assess for every topic. So we do quite a bit of assessing. I find it takes a lot of time.

This new teacher felt that assessment was very time-consuming. In contrast, the next teacher felt happy about the amount of assessment that was required:

> With assessment, the school's made it so easy. We have targets for each child, it's fantastic and that's the only thing we've got to submit. We have the assessment target sheets and we fill them in as and when children achieve the targets.

So far, many of the examples that we have looked at have been about summative assessment: marking and levelling written work, for example. Summative assessment involves assessing pupils' work, the outcomes of which may be used to develop ideas about what to plan for future lessons. However, it does not involve considering how to meet the needs of individual pupils. This is an important aspect of assessment and one with which you will be familiar. Formative assessment is also of great importance if you are to help the pupils achieve their potential, but what do we mean by formative assessment? According to Black and Williams (1998) 'assessment' refers to those activities which provide information to be used as feedback to modify teaching and learning activities. They consider that such assessment becomes formative assessment when: 'the evidence is actually used to adapt the teaching work to meet the needs' (Black and Wiliams 1998). So, if you are assessing your pupils and using that information to adapt your work or to plan your teaching with the aim of meeting the needs of individual pupils, then you are involved in formative assessment. You may not be as aware of how much of this kind of assessment you are doing, as in the next case:

> I'm actually doing more than I realize in terms of assessment. I assess all the time. I'm always thinking, 'Well, that hasn't been covered so well, so let's go over it tomorrow', and I use assessment in my planning. You know, I'm always thinking about what the children know and how I can take them on further. So I'm actually assessing all the time without realizing.

In the above example, the beginning teacher was putting into practice a cycle of ongoing formative assessment which informed planning, without being necessarily conscious of this process all the time: assessment was already well embedded in their overall daily practice. It may help you to think about this day to day evaluation and assessment in order to realize how much formative assessment for children's learning you are already doing in this way. As well as assessing children's achievements, the point made by the teacher above about how to 'take them further' is a crucial one and underlies principles of assessment for learning set out by the Assessment Reform Group (see website references for further information). As a teacher, you will need to be able to identify pupil errors and misconceptions and set targets which make clear the next steps that the children should take to improve their work. As part of this, you can also encourage the children to start assessing and reviewing their own and others' work: self- and peer-assessment is an important part of the learning process.

As well as assessing children's work and target setting, you also need to record your assessments. As one of the teachers we spoke to commented:

> I can assess the children, that's not a problem, but I think that every teacher has their own individual way of evaluating work and assessing work and I just need to work out a way to do it and record it for myself. I've got it in my head but I couldn't show it to anybody. I want something quick, clear and useful. It might take me a while to develop, but that's one area I do need to work on.

The teacher quoted above was happy about assessing the children, but had not devised a way of recording the assessment details. It is important that you do record assessment information as it may be needed by other teachers within the school, by the headteacher or you may need to draw on it when talking to parents; it is not sufficient to keep such details 'in your head'. Make sure that you know what your school policy is on marking and record keeping, so that your own records match those of other teachers, although of course you can supplement these with others of your own. Don't forget, if you have the help of teaching assistants, they may assist you with this too; for instance, they may be able to record children's responses in the shared part of a lesson or in guided groups.

If you find that assessing children's work is taking up a lot of time, then you may need to spend some time thinking about how much work and which work you assess. It is not necessary to assess every piece of work that every child does. There may be certain subject areas that your school requires you to assess more than others, such as literacy and numeracy, but there may be some areas where you can choose what is important to assess in detail and what is not so important. As one teacher commented at the beginning of the second year in teaching:

> I'm far more geared up now into what needs to be assessed and what doesn't need to be assessed. So as well as being able to assess work more quickly, I can actually decide which work I need to assess and which work I don't.

Assessment is often carried out on a year group or whole school basis; for example, moderation and levelling of written work. This will also help you to get better at assessing children's learning and make it more of a shared process.

Key findings and action points

We have considered in some detail in this chapter:

- diversity in the inclusive classroom;
- managing behaviour;
- assessment issues.

As we have seen, beginning teachers are more likely to highlight what they perceive as the challenges of working with special educational needs, or difficult behaviour, and to overlook other equally important issues, such as gender or working with gifted and talented children.

We saw that there are a range of ways in which you can obtain help and guidance, including observing experienced teachers and working with teaching assistants and other colleagues, as well as making the most of other internal and external expertise.

When assessing children's learning, many new teachers worry about the process as well as the possible overload of assessment and record keeping. They tend to see it as something separate from the teaching and learning going on in the classroom. We looked at the importance of finding out about and working with the school's assessment policy, and focusing on your daily, formative evaluations of children's learning, rather than always on summative aspects such as marking and levelling.

Action points

- Try to remember the needs of all your pupils, rather than just a few individuals or groups.
- Be aware of your own areas of bias and preconception and try not to let these get in the way of relating to all your pupils as equally as possible.

- Talk to and observe experienced teachers to see a range of differentiation and class management strategies.
- Draw on the expertise of specialist units or teachers in the school, as well as outside experts, such as speech and language specialists or minority ethnic support teachers.
- Work alongside teaching assistants to help support learning, behaviour and assessment.
- Use your ongoing evaluations and assessment of children's learning to support your planning and teaching and enhance pupils' learning.

Concluding discussion

An important underlying issue which we have highlighted in this chapter is that of teachers' attitudes and preconceptions. All teachers have their own areas of bias, not just beginning teachers, but it is very easy for these to be confirmed through seeing certain individual children, or groups of pupils, as problematic. It's most important to keep an open mind as far as possible, and try to see the positive potential of all your pupils: setting high expectations will lead to children living up to these rather than confirming your concerns. At the heart of teaching and learning are the positive relationships and interactions between you and your class and it is on these that you can build.

Further reading and useful website links

Black, P., Harrison, C., Lee, C., Marshall, B. and Wiliam, D. (2003) *Assessment for Learning: Putting it into Practice*. Buckingham: Open University Press.

Clarke, S. (2001) *Unlocking Formative Assessment: Practical Strategies for Enhancing Pupils' Learning in the Primary Classroom*. London: Hodder and Stoughton, www.shirleyclarke-education.org

Cowley, S. (2001) *Getting the Buggers to Behave*. London: Continuum.

Pollard, A. and Bourne, J. (1994) *Teaching and Learning in the Primary School*. London: Routledge in association with the Open University.

Roffey, S. (2004) *The New Teacher's Survival Guide to Behaviour*. London: Paul Chapman.

Torrance, H. and Pryor, J. (1998) *Investigating Formative Assessment*. Buckingham: Open University Press.

Weston, C. (2004) *The Inclusive Classroom: A Practical Guide for Teachers*. Exeter: Learning Matters.

There are a number of websites which you may also find useful, such as: www.aaia.org.uk/assessment

www.behaviour4learning.ac.uk
www.qca.org.uk/3.html
www.teachernet.gov.uk/research/researchtopics/ethnicity
www.teachernet.gov.uk/wholeschool/sen

7
Professional issues: relationships with adults

This chapter builds on the previous two by focusing on some of the professional relationships involved in the primary teacher's role. These are crucial as they can either become a source of support to the beginning teacher or be perceived as a barrier to their development. The chapter will cover working with induction mentors and other teachers, teaching assistants and parents, and it will look at the varying relationships built by the beginning teachers in our research.

Introduction

A crucial aspect of the primary teacher's role is the relationships they will form with other adults, in particular other teachers, mentors and teaching assistants. As we will demonstrate in this chapter, these relationships are not just an add-on, but are central to teachers' work and support, particularly in the first years of teaching when new teachers are still learning so much. They often need to look to others with more experience for guidance. We have already seen in the first part of the book how important the support and the knowledge gained from other teachers were to the four case study teachers. In this chapter we will also see some examples of the role of the headteacher, induction mentors and other staff in supporting new teachers, and the professional relationships that new teachers built with them.

With the remodelling agenda, the role of teaching assistants in the school is growing in importance and scope. Trainee teachers are already learning how to plan to work with teaching assistants (TAs) in the classroom, and this develops more in the induction year and beyond. In this chapter we will look at how the case study teachers and some other teachers in our research worked with TAs and developed productive working relationships with them.

Beginning teachers in our research often expressed concerns about how they would relate to parents and sometimes imagined 'worst case scenarios' in which parents complained about their work. In this chapter we will draw mainly on the experiences of the case study teachers to illustrate how they developed confidence in relating to parents.

Working with induction mentors

In your first year of teaching you will be entitled to support from an induction mentor, who will often be your first port of call if there are any problems, but who will also take the lead in organizing and monitoring your induction programme throughout the year. Research into induction support (Simco 2003; Bubb and Earley 2004a) has identified that this support can be variable, and that the degree of input from the induction mentor can be crucial in terms of the beginning teacher's professional development.

Let's have a look at the role the mentor played in the professional development of the teachers in our research, starting with Cathryn. At the start of her first year, Cathryn was beginning to see the benefits of sharing the planning for the Year 1 classes with her mentor:

> My mentor's good. She's the other Year 1 teacher and we roughly plan together, not exactly, because she has the lower ability Year 1 and I have the higher ones, but we plan the outline of what we're doing together.

But by the end of her first year, Cathryn could see much more fully how supportive her mentor had been and how much she had learnt from her:

> My mentor has been brilliant, she has helped me so much. I can go to her at any time and she's always willing to offer help. With the planning … she had all the experience and knew what to do.

As we saw in Chapter 4, Abbey found the staff at her school highly supportive, which enabled her to try things out and make mistakes without fear of criticism. Central to this support seemed to be her mentor:

> I see my mentor regularly, but I can see her any time. She observes me and gives me really good feedback, and all the staff are really helpful.

What Cathryn's and Abbey's mentors had in common was their availability: both new teachers mentioned being able to see their mentors 'at any time'. What was also really important though was the mentors' approachability. Many other beginning teachers stressed the importance of their mentors being both available and approachable, even if they did not need to seek their help that often. Knowing the mentors were there to call on as and when help was needed gave Cathryn and Abbey a sense of security.

The nature of support mentors gave the new teachers in our studies varied. In addition to the practical and emotional support they offered, beginning teachers learnt professionally from their mentors, for instance Cathryn in terms of planning and Abbey from the regular observation and feedback she received. These aspects were frequently mentioned by other new teachers as well. Gina reported that she received regular practical advice from her mentor. When asked about what aspects of teaching her mentor had helped her with, she replied:

> Oh everything … Really, she explained so much about her reasons for doing so many things, and that was such a help because, rather than just observing her doing things, I actually began to understand far more about why she did things.

Gina observed her mentor teaching, but the most valuable part to her was the way her mentor was able to explain how and why she did things in a particular way, such as grouping children. The relationship she had built with her mentor was crucial in enabling this to happen. It was a relationship built on mutual trust: Gina trusted her mentor to give her reliable advice and the mentor trusted Gina to take her advice seriously. The process of working alongside experienced teachers and learning with them and from them, as Gina did, is recognized as a vital resource for beginning teachers (e.g. Simco 2003). The explanations that mentors and other teachers can give to new teachers about their practice are cited as a particularly valuable way of passing on experience and helping new teachers understand the reasons behind choices made in the classroom.

In a recent study looking at the transfer of good practice (Fielding et al. 2005), it was found that teachers tended to extend and refine their existing repertoire of practice, rather than to precisely copy the practice of other teachers. The term 'joint practice development' is therefore used to describe the work of two teachers, in this case the mentor and new teacher, who are working together with the aim of developing the practice of one of these teachers.

However, in some cases the designated mentor does not always fulfil their expected role. This problem was highlighted in a recent study of induction and early teaching by Bubb and Earley (2004a) and we also found the same issue occurring in relation to some NQTs' in our research, for instance as the following new teacher says:

> No, we don't have any meetings and [the mentor] she's observed me twice, but she was late for both sessions, and the feedback took about three minutes. She never comes and just asks, 'How do you feel?'

There was a positive outcome in this case, because a senior teacher un-officially took on the role of induction mentor when it was realized that the NQT was not being observed:

> I suppose the deputy head has taken on the role of mentor, it's her I go to, to discuss anything. In fact, she's just observed me this week, and she went completely by the book. She observed for the set time and debriefed me properly, she has been a real help.

However, the absence of effective mentoring in the early part of the induction year made this teacher anxious about what would happen in their second year of teaching:

> I would like to think I'll be given some support next year, by the school generally … but [the mentor] she's retiring this year so she's not going to be there to help, but I do think there should be some sort of support for second year teachers.

A national pilot on the early career development of teachers identified the importance of continued mentoring in the second and third years of teaching, but unfortunately the funding to support this was discontinued (Moor et al. 2005). However, rather than just rely on the support you may and should get in your induction year and beyond, it's also important for you as beginning teachers to make use of other sources of support, both within and outside the school. Induction consultants (see the Teacher Training Agency (TTA) website www.tta.gov.uk/induction) stress the need for new teachers to develop skills of self-reliance and the ability to take a proactive role in their own professional development, and we saw this as important in the case study teachers, in their first year of teaching.

Before turning to the role that other teachers play in the development of beginning teachers, have a look at Activity 7.1. This activity focuses on the nature of the relationship built between mentors and new teachers.

Activity 7.1

First, look back at the quotes in this section of the chapter and identify the ways in which the mentors helped the new teachers. What kind of support did they provide?

Now think about your own induction mentor or, if you are just starting your NQT year, about a mentor you had on teaching practice. Note the ways in which you found them helpful. What kind of help or support did they give you? How effective was it? Why was this?

Hopefully this activity will have highlighted for you the kinds of support you find helpful and effective in your professional development, and why. This in turn will help you in developing a fruitful dialogue with your mentor. Remember that building a successful working relationship is a crucial part of working effectively with your mentor and this is a two-way process.

Working with other teachers

> The school is fantastic, they give me all the support I need
>
> (Abbey)

> It's all fine, I'm really well supported, I can talk to other staff about any problems or issues

The above quotes by Abbey and another teacher are typical of many from beginning teachers about the whole school support that they received. As with mentoring, the approachability of staff was an important factor which gave new teachers confidence that they could ask for help if needed, as in the example below:

> I was given lots of support. I had two hours non-contact time per week. People didn't bother me unless I asked for it, but if I did ask for help, I was given whatever support I needed. Like, I wanted to observe a PE specialist, so I asked about that and when I'd observed them I asked them to come and observe me to tell me how I was doing and how I could improve. I was always given the help I needed.

This teacher, looking back on the first year of teaching, was not afraid to take the initiative in asking for help. Having identified an area needing support – PE – and the need to observe experienced teachers in this subject the teacher had also realized that they would benefit most by being observed as well. Other new teachers to whom we spoke were concerned about sometimes being seen to be needing too much support, or felt that their questions may have been seen as a sign of not being sufficiently prepared. The following quotes illustrate how some beginning teachers also felt as though they were a burden to other, more experienced, teachers and how some teachers were reluctant to ask questions in case their questions were seen as trivial:

> My colleagues were very supportive, however sometimes I felt guilty in taking up their already precious time. I did not necessarily feel that I was on my own, more frustrated with the situation that I was in.

It's just that sometimes when you want to ask silly questions you feel a bit daft asking them.

In the second case, the teacher was particularly anxious not to be perceived as 'daft' by other teachers or the head. In fact the role of the headteacher in setting the ethos of the school can be crucial, and can set the tone for the way other teachers in the school relate to new teachers. In a minority of cases among the new teachers to whom we talked, the attitudes and behaviour of senior management were perceived as negative:

> I'm given a lot of support from our department, which is great, but not from management, they seem to be too far removed from the classroom. I don't feel as if I get as much support from them as I would like

> I was given too much support; it was as if they didn't trust me to do what I had to do. Sometimes I would realize that the head was watching me, when at first I didn't know she was, I felt she never really let me get on with things ... the head was notorious in terms of expecting great things from teachers, she'd really push us. She was overpowering, it's things like, I would go into my cupboard and I'd see she'd been in the cupboard and she'd maybe leave a note saying, 'You shouldn't store such and such in this cupboard'. She seemed to be always snooping around and always be there. She was just so unapproachable.

In the first case, the senior staff appeared too distant from the new teacher, although the other teachers were seen as supportive. In the other example, the new teacher felt over-scrutinized, observed in a negative way, which undermined any feeling of trust. Headteachers who behave in this negative kind of way or show lack of support and trust in their staff have been labelled as 'rogue' heads (Bubb and Earley 2004a) and fortunately they seem to be, very much, in a minority. As we saw with mentors, the key component was approachability, which was lacking in these examples. When building relationships between teachers one important factor is that both partners should be perceived by each other as non-threatening and feel at ease to talk about their concerns as well as their achievements. When a non-threatening environment is not present, the teachers involved are less likely to build trusting relationships (Fielding et al. 2005).

Cathryn had a positive experience of support in her school, which was very much led from the top:

I'm very happy with the support. My head is the sort of person you can approach whenever you want to, and if he's got a problem with what you're doing he always goes about it in a nice way … In fact the whole school will offer help, so I think it's really the support from my mentor and from my other teaching colleagues.

Here's another example of how a headteacher took the lead in monitoring the development of an NQT and providing constructive feedback, which was then followed by other staff:

The head was great; we'd meet each week and see how I was getting on, and talk about where I was going and what I had achieved. The other staff, they were fantastic as well. I worked with another member of staff; a lot of people didn't get on with her, but I rather liked her. She used to say what was on her mind, and once you accepted that she wasn't getting at you personally it was all right. She gave me a lot of helpful advice.

We can see from the last two quotes that the way teachers give advice and support is an important factor in whether the new teacher is able to receive this feedback and act on it. For example, Cathryn stressed that the head of her school dealt with any problems 'in a nice way', so she felt he was being positive rather than critical. In the second example, the beginning teacher was able to take the advice of another teacher in a positive way, but was aware that other teachers found this particular member of staff rather abrupt and direct. In both of these cases, a trusting relationship between the head and the new teacher was developing, with both partners having confidence in each other. This is another important ingredient that needs to be present in a successful working relationship. The ability to defuse potentially negative feedback and not take it personally is also important, and something which some new teachers find hard when they are inexperienced or feeling low in terms of their own confidence, as the next examples illustrate:

Another thing that wasn't covered on the course was dealing with other teachers. They can be very difficult, not so much for me, as I'm used to unpredictable behaviour, but for some of the other younger girls, who are straight from college and haven't done anything else. I've seen them upset by the abruptness of some of the staff, and it's ruined their days.

I team teach: we've got a two form entry and my main problem in the first term was a sort of personality clash with another tutor. I found it difficult to get my point of view across; he was a bit chauvinistic and always thought he knew better. And he made me feel like I was just this new teacher and my ideas weren't as good as his. But now I've gained confidence and that's made things easier. I've got more confidence now and say, 'Well, look, I really think this should work, let's give it a go,' and to be fair on me, a lot of my ideas I've had have worked really well.

As in any work situation, much of the dynamic between teachers boils down to personal relationships and the ability to give and take, and this is something that develops over time as teachers gain experience and become more confident in themselves, as shown in the above quotes. The main thing is to try not to be defensive or assume that others are setting out to be critical. Sometimes advice is meant well but not expressed in the most diplomatic way. Remember, experienced teachers sometimes feel threatened by the arrival of a new teacher brimming full of enthusiasm and new ideas. As one NQT put it, 'I was this new kid on the block with strange ideas!' Be sensitive to that and try to be aware of other teachers' feelings too.

Very similar issues arose in relation to working with and developing relationships with teaching assistants and parents, although the power relations can be rather different, as we shall see.

Working with teaching assistants

When we looked at the experiences and perceptions of beginning teachers, one of the main differences some identified between working with other teachers in the school and working alongside teaching assistants was the reversal of the balance of power. While some new teachers tended to feel in a lower status position compared to experienced teachers, they perceived themselves to be in a managerial position in relation to TAs, and this sometimes created its own problems. Let's look at the way Abbey and Cathryn talked about working with teaching assistants:

> I found it hard initially because I felt I wasn't confident about telling them what to do and I'm not confrontational, so I found that difficult, but things are getting easier now as I'm gaining more confidence.
>
> (Abbey)

> There was nothing on the course about it [working with TAs]; it was my own experience as a classroom assistant, and with me being a mature student. I can imagine that some of the younger NQTs could find it a problem, especially if the teaching assistant is a lot older

than them, but for me, I had a clear idea of the sort of things I wanted her to do, and it's worked out really well.

(Cathryn)

There was quite a difference between Abbey and Cathryn in terms of their confidence in working with TAs initially, partly due to the difference in their ages and prior experience. Abbey was an example of a 'younger NQT' who found it hard to ask an older teaching assistant to do things for her. In Cathryn's case, because she was older and had been a TA herself, she had a clear idea about a TA's role and also had confidence in relating to the TA she worked with. Prior experience as a teaching assistant was another important factor which resulted in Fatou having confidence when developing a working relationship with her TA. Her change of role from TA to teacher, however, brought with it its own problems, as she explained:

> She's [my TA] an asset, she's really fab. I've known her for years. We used to work together as classroom assistants and she's just brilliant. It was a bit strange for us working together as teacher and classroom assistant, when we'd worked together as classroom assistants in the past, but we soon got used to it, and it works really well ... It was weird at first ... I felt that some of the assistants saw me as I'd sort of gone over to the other side and they thought of me differently, but now that I'm in there teaching and they see how I am, they realize that I haven't changed. I've just become a teacher, but I'm still me.

(Fatou)

Although Fatou had a head start in terms of being familiar with the role and knowing the teaching assistants themselves, she had to prove that she had not changed or 'gone over to the other side'. Notice the way that Fatou talked about 'working together' with her TA; she had a particular perception of the balance of power and of the partnership she wanted to develop. Other new teachers who had been classroom assistants themselves used similar ways of describing the relationship:

> I'd been an LSA myself, so I knew how they worked, and I was used to being with staff and working with staff in school.

In comparison, it was the managerial aspect of the relationship with teaching assistants that younger teachers often emphasized and worried about. As with Abbey, phrases like 'telling them what to do' cropped up in many of the interviews we had with new teachers:

> At the beginning I wasn't getting on with [the TA] very well, but now I have a different one. I found it quite hard to tell her what to do. That was a real problem with my first teaching assistant, because she was a lot older than me and she had been at the school a long time. But things are better now, and I find it easier to tell this teaching assistant what to do.

> Managing my TA, I've got a new TA this year and I've got more TA help which is good because I can get odd jobs done with her. But I do feel I've advanced in that area because I'm able to manage her better now.

> I didn't like to put on [the TA] at first, I felt awkward asking her to sharpen pencils and that, but she's said that's what she's there for, and it's easier now.

All the above NQTs felt that the situation became easier as the year went on; in the third example, the teaching assistant herself made it easier by reassuring the teacher about her role. As another beginning teacher said, 'You just build up a relationship with [TAs] and that just takes time.'

Another aspect which was exemplified by the above quotes was the way in which some new teachers saw the role of the TA as one of doing 'odd jobs', sharpening pencils and so on. Some teaching assistants may have seen their job in this way as well; for instance, the TA who said 'that's what she's there for', and some TAs may see their role as only marginally concerned with children's learning. However, the position of the teaching assistant is changing rapidly and some TAs are taking on far more central roles in the classroom as part of a larger team of adults supporting children's needs. For some time now, learning support assistants have worked with groups of children to provide phonics and general literacy support. Others have worked with individual children with special educational needs, and these TAs often have specialized training and expertise.

There are growing opportunities for TAs to become higher level teaching assistants (HLTAs) or to take degree courses which may lead to qualified teacher status, so there is far more of a continuum now than in the past. Schools are involving teaching assistants in the planning process and seeing their responsibilities in a much wider way than before (see Drake et al. 2004 for further information on these changes). In addition, the role of the TA is growing yet further with the introduction of workforce remodelling and protected non-contact time for teachers, as we shall see in Chapter 12.

The following example shows a new teacher who had a limited view of a teaching assistant's role, which was clearly not shared by other teachers in the school:

> I have had a problem with my TA, she reported me to the deputy head. The thing was, basically, when I used to talk to the class as a group, she'd be there listening and not doing anything else, but I didn't want her sitting listening to me telling the class a story, I wanted her to be doing cutting out or whatever when I was doing that, but no one backed me up on it, so that was a bit difficult, but she's brilliant with the kids.

Unfortunately, in this case no one had explained to the beginning teacher what the teaching assistant could be doing instead of 'cutting out'. For instance, a far more valuable use of the TA's time and expertise during shared reading could have been to record the children's responses, thus giving the teacher some useful information on individual children. The fact that this TA was 'brilliant with the kids' gave a clue as to a more productive way in which the teacher could have made more of the TA's skills to enhance pupil learning.

In contrast, some of the beginning teachers we talked to were acknowledging the expertise of teaching assistants and encouraging them to take on a wider role in the classroom. For example, the following NQT was fortunate to have the help of a TA to provide specialized support to an individual pupil with special educational needs; however, while in the class, the teacher was able to allow the TA to more fully support other groups of children:

> Now I have a full-time TA as we've got this girl from a special school and she needs a full-time teaching assistant, and she's great. She helps out so much with groups of children so I don't always have to be with the lowest set.

Other new teachers were beginning to plan for teaching assistants and to realize that they and other adults in the class could fulfil an important role in supporting children's learning:

> There's a lot of planning for them. I've got to write down all of the activities I want them to do, and I plan the activities for the children ... I seem to be writing down small activities all of the time, and it takes a long time to plan the classroom assistant's work, as the groups might be doing very different work and I can't write down the same for each classroom assistant.

> It's not an easy thing to do, but I have a link book which the TAs read so they know what they're doing, and all the parents can read and know what they're doing and I find that helps a lot.

As can be seen from these and many of the other examples, there was still some uncertainty around planning for teaching assistants and the feeling that it could involve a lot of work. If you are in this position yourself, try Activity 7.2.

Activity 7.2

Find out what the policy is in your school regarding how teachers work with teaching assistants and what the TAs' roles and responsibilities are. Also make sure you know how many teaching assistants there are, who they are and what their specific responsibilities might be.

If you have a teaching assistant assigned to your class, make sure you know when they work: is it a regular day or time, or do they share their time between your class and another class? Are they assigned to support a particular child? If so what is their role with that child? Find out what type of work they have done before and if they have worked with the class before. Also find out what the TA feels they are good at and what they enjoy doing in the classroom.

Now think about how you can make the most of the TA's time in your class. For example, you could plan for them to work with one group during activity time in literacy and numeracy, but try to vary this so that all the groups can benefit from working with the teaching assistant.

How will you and the teaching assistant work together? How will you build an effective partnership? How will you plan for their work time? Arrange to meet with the teaching assistant so you can discuss, and ensure you are both clear about, your roles. Remember how important it is to build effective working relationships with colleagues, especially if you will be working together in the same room for much of the time.

As with relationships with other teachers, be sensitive to the needs of the teaching assistants you work with and remember that they may feel just as anxious as you about meeting and working with a new teacher.

Relationships with parents

Anxieties in relationships with parents were also very evident among the new teachers to whom we talked, and this was also reflected in the questionnaire responses (see Table 5.1). As we saw in Chapter 4, Abbey regarded her relationships with parents as one of her biggest challenges in the first year of teaching and this feeling was shared by many others, as the following examples demonstrate:

> I think dealing with parents [was my biggest challenge]. I was very nervous to begin with; I never knew what they were going to say and I never knew what to say to them, but now I'm far more confident.

> I'm not quite as scared of parents as I was. I found it really daunting before with parents, but I'm getting more confidence with them now.

As with teaching assistants, we found a difference between those younger teachers who had not worked in schools before and those who had been teaching assistants and were used to dealing with parents in a different role. For example, compare Abbey and Gina's comments on this:

> I've also got more confidence with parents; that's certainly growing, and that has made things easier this term. I've not been so worried about talking to parents.
>
> (Abbey)

> I suppose I was happy to deal with parents because I'd often talked to parents as a teaching assistant, and it just didn't worry me. Also I was a mature student and I think when you're young, that sort of thing bothers you more.
>
> (Gina)

In spite of their different starting points, almost all the teachers who told us about their early worries and fears about talking to parents also stressed how these had been overcome as their confidence had grown during their first year in teaching. Some teachers reported a change as they gained experience of communicating with and reporting to parents:

> At the first parents' evening I was the teacher who was running most behind time. I was so late leaving the caretakers were waiting to lock up. But by the second parents' evening I'd really learned to keep on time far better.
>
> (Fatou)

> I've gained experience of writing reports and of parent's evenings. I was very unsure about both of those things before, but now that I have had the experience and gone through it I feel far more confident in those areas.

Parents' evenings were a particular source of worry, which often proved unfounded, as this teacher reported:

> We did lots of role-play and lots of report writing on the course, but I was still really worried when it came to parents' evening, but now I've done one and it was a doddle really. You realize that the parents are just normal people. Before the parents' evening, I worried about the kind of reaction I'd get from parents, but it was fine.

Just as Abbey, in Chapter 3, did not feel like a real teacher until her second year when she was in a position where she could advise an NQT, some teachers did not feel confident with parents until they moved into their second year of teaching:

> I feel far more confident about that [parents] now. At first I was really nervous with parents, I didn't know what to say, but now, I suppose because also I'm in my second year, they treat me as a teacher rather than an NQT and I am far more confident.

> I've gained more confidence when talking to parents. Last year they knew I was new but now I feel really quite established in the school.

However, many teachers still retained some anxiety about parents, even after their first year in teaching and some successful parents' evenings under their belt – as one said, 'I'm still not sure what to say and what not to say'; teachers further on in their careers felt much more secure in this area. Let's finish this section by looking at aspects of their teaching which Gina and Fatou thought they had progressed in by the time they were three years into their teaching careers:

> Liaising with parents, that's partly due to my age and my past experience. But also I'm far more confident now and also with things like assemblies and helping with shows, that's one area I really enjoy.
>
> (Gina)

> I'm quite opinionated in meetings and with parents and I feel confident to take part in discussions and put my point of view forward, and I'm not afraid to be assertive with difficult parents. And now having moved down to nursery, that's been another boost to my confidence because I've done home visits to most of all the parents of the children I've got in my class, so I've already started to build a relationship with these parents and I feel very on top of it and very in control.
>
> (Fatou)

As with relationships with teachers, relationships with parents take time to develop. Fatou had moved a long way from her first experience of a parents' evening when she ran so late, she was now building new skills in doing home visits for her early years children. Gina was also enlarging her repertoire of skills to include a wider audience through assemblies and shows, thus reaching and relating to parents in different ways. Above all, both teachers felt on top of what they were doing and full of confidence.

Key findings and action points

In this chapter, we discussed working relationships with other adults in the school. These were:

- induction mentors;
- other teachers;
- teaching assistants;
- parents.

Induction mentors were seen by the new teachers as a potentially vital source of support for professional development. As well as generally being 'supportive and approachable', what the new teachers in our studies found to be effective included opportunities for:

- joint planning;
- observation of their mentor with discussion afterwards;
- mentors explaining their practice and why they did what they did;
- observation by their mentor, with constructive feedback afterwards.

Other teachers were also an important source of support and guidance, in much the same way as mentors could be, and this tended to be most effective when led by the headteacher or senior teachers. The way teachers gave and received feedback could be a difficult area for new teachers.

Some of the beginning teachers we talked to felt that it had been difficult to prepare for working with TAs during their training and that this was something they had to learn 'on the job'. Those who had been teaching assistants themselves tended to be more confident in their relationships with TAs. Remember that the role of the teaching assistant is currently changing and it is important to check what the policy is in your school.

We saw that relating to parents caused anxiety for many of the new teachers in our study, but their confidence did grow once they had had more experience, for instance, of parents' evenings. Once the beginning teachers had become more established in their school, often in their second year of teaching, this aspect seemed to become easier.

Action points

- Identify colleagues in or out of school who can provide support and advice; extend and vary your networks of support as much as possible.
- Be sensitive to others and try not to be overly defensive when receiving advice or feedback which may be more critical.
- Learn how to be self-reliant and use your initiative in asking for help rather than waiting for it to be offered.
- Include TAs in your planning and assessment of children as widely as possible, acknowledging their expertise and their preferred areas of work. Work with them to build partnerships.
- Try not to be afraid of parents. As one teacher said, 'Parents are people too!'

Concluding discussion

Some of the concerns that arose about working relationships in school came down to the importance of personal and social skills. New teachers need to develop sensitivity, self-reliance and initiative when working with parents and colleagues in school and to be aware that experience will bring greater confidence. Time spent in school actually working alongside other professionals and communicating with parents will help beginning teachers to develop these skills.

At the time of writing, the renegotiation of teachers' and teaching assistants' roles and responsibilities is a discussion point in schools with the introduction of workforce remodelling. These changes will take time to bed down and, as with any change, schools will interpret remodelling in different ways. There are a number of other initiatives on the horizon which will affect the ways in which professionals learn to work with each other (e.g. the Children's Agenda). The kinds of challenges which the new teachers in our study faced are likely to be ones to which you can relate. But there will be others: for instance some of you may already be working with education professionals from outside school and/or from other agencies (e.g. perhaps working together to support a pupil with challenging behaviour). Remember, working with others depends on building good working relationships and this was at the heart of what the new teachers in our study found.

Further reading and useful website links

Bubb, S. and Earley, P. (2004a) *Leading and Managing Continuing Professional Development: Developing People; Developing Schools*. London: Paul Chapman.

Simco, N. (2003) *Succeeding in the Induction Year*, 2nd edn. Exeter: Learning Matters.

Thomas, G. (1992) *Effective Classroom Teamwork: Support or Intrusion?* London: Routledge.

Vincent, K., Cremin, H. and Thomas, G. (2005) *Teachers and Assistants working Together*. Maidenhead: Open University Press.

Wolfendale, S. (1992) *Involving Parents in Schools*. London: Cassell.

Some useful websites are as follows:

www.teachernet.gov.uk/wholeschool/teachingassistants

www.tta.gov.uk/induction

www.nfer.ac.uk

PART 3
Reflecting on practice: towards a model of professional learning

This third part of the book takes a different approach to Parts 1 and 2 by examining the findings of the earlier chapters and looking for wider explanations. A model of teachers' professional learning is introduced in Chapters 8 and 9 to help you reflect on your own practice and stage in professional development. The model separates learning into two broad areas: learning in relation to the acquisition of teaching skills and learning in relation to managing the demands of teaching. The model of professional learning is presented and explained initially through the experiences of Abbey and Cathryn (in Chapter 8) and then through the experiences of Fatou and Gina (in Chapter 9). We draw on aspects of these four teachers' professional learning to help explain the model, as you will already be familiar with their experiences from the earlier chapters in the book. The activities aim to help you to use the model to reflect on your own experiences, as well as to analyse your strengths and areas for further development. Practical ways of improving practice are also suggested.

Again in this part of the book we use the experiences and voices of the new teachers introduced in the first two parts of the book. In addition, in Chapter 10, we also draw on the findings of a study of the recruitment and retention of primary teachers. We sent questionnaires to all primary teachers who had trained on a PGCE programme at one institution during the 1990s, asking them about their current jobs and teaching careers, whether they were still in teaching and reasons for staying in or dropping out of teaching. With the help of the university's alumni association, we spent some time tracing the teachers, and eventually tracked down 219 (46.7 percent of the total). We also carried out in-depth follow-up interviews with a sample of ten teachers and then a further 22 who became the cohort study (32 in total, see Appendix for further details).

Throughout this book we have drawn on the experiences and voices of new teachers which we hope has provided a context within which you can understand your own experiences. In this third part of the book we take this one step further by using the model to help us explore the experiences of Abbey, Cathryn, Fatou and Gina as a way of supporting reflection on, and helping you realistically plan for, your own professional development.

8
Introducing a model of professional learning

This chapter introduces a way of looking at and understanding early professional development. Looking back to the case studies, issues surrounding aspects of teaching skills and other professional demands are analysed with reference to a model of professional learning. Unlike other models which tend to present professional development as a linear process, this model highlights the impact of broader issues such as personal and professional demands on professional development.

Introduction

In the first part of this book, we saw how the four new teachers, Abbey, Cathryn, Fatou and Gina, developed professionally in different ways, due to a variety of different reasons, as they started out in their new careers. Many new teachers said to us that it is only when you are responsible for your own class and you are 'doing it for real', that learning really takes off. What did they mean by this? Professional learning doesn't just start when you begin your first teaching post. If you are reading this having just finished your training, or are just about to start out in teaching, you will no doubt know that you have already learnt a tremendous amount on your initial training programme. However, you enter a new phase of learning once you leave your initial training behind you. One new teacher described beginning primary teaching in their first post in the following way:

> Well, it's like riding a bike. When you first start, you're thinking, I must push this pedal, then I must push the other pedal, and once you can ride well, you start looking around and seeing what's going on around you. It was the same for me. In my first year, I was so involved with what I was doing, planning the lessons and sticking to the plans, without really deviating from them, but by the second year, it was easier and more natural. I was more confident and I started to evaluate what I was doing as I was going along. I was more aware of what I was doing.

This analogy for the acquisition of teaching skills during the early years of teaching is a useful one, and one which we will discuss later in this chapter. However, as you will know by now, learning to teach is far more complicated than learning to ride a bike. In addition to developing teaching skills, new teachers must also learn how to cope with a range of professional demands, such as planning, record keeping and assessment. When we traced new teachers' progress during the first few years in their new career, we were able to identify patterns in their professional development and learning. In this chapter, we will introduce you to these patterns and to a way of thinking about your professional learning in the early years of your career, which links the acquisition of teaching skills with the ability to cope with the other professional demands which are likely to be placed on you. In order to try to understand the stages of professional learning, we will focus on the development of two of the new teachers, whom we first met in Part 1 of this book, Abbey and Cathryn.

The acquisition of teaching skills

As we have seen with Abbey, Cathryn, Fatou and Gina, professional learning is complex, but understanding the stages new teachers tend to pass through can be helpful. From our research, we were able to identify four stages in the acquisition of teaching skills: survival, coping, exploring and proficiency (see Figure 8.1).

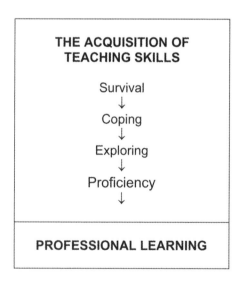

Figure 8.1 Stages in the acquisition of teaching skills

The quote using the bike metaphor encapsulated the way in which many new teachers described to us their experiences as they began teaching. But before we look more closely at what this teacher said, have a go at Activity 8.1 which aims to start you thinking about the stages experienced by Abbey and Cathryn as they acquired teaching skills.

Activity 8.1

Turn back to Chapter 4 and look again at the first section of that chapter which is entitled: 'What happened to the four teachers in their first three years?'

Read Abbey's story again and as you read it, keep in mind the four stages (i.e. survival, coping, exploring and proficiency). Can you identify when she reached each stage?

Now read Cathryn's story. Do you think she reached any of the stages at the same time as Abbey? If so, why do you think this was? Try to identify the factors which affected the two teachers' acquisition of teaching skills.

Now let's go back to the quote at the beginning of this chapter. Although not a perfect analogy, we can use the idea of learning to ride a bike to help us think about beginning teaching in much the same way as this teacher did. When we learn to ride a bike we are often given a lot of support, for example we use stabilizers, and some of us start by having to think about every single push of the pedal. As we progress and no longer have this support, we may wobble at first and sometimes fall off, but once we get the hang of it we're off. We can then further develop our skills in all sorts of ways, for instance, by learning mountain biking. Figure 8.2 uses the analogy of riding a bike to describe and explain the characteristics of stages in the acquisition of teaching skills.

Beginning primary teaching

↓

'When you first start, you're thinking I must push this pedal, then I must push the other pedal . . . in my first year, I was so involved with what I was doing, planning the lessons and sticking to the plans, without really deviating from them' – in other words, at first she was just *surviving*. Abbey was similarly just surviving teaching at the end of her first term. She had quickly realized that she had a lot to learn in terms of teaching skills.

↓

Figure 8.2 *cont.*

But before long, you don't have to think about each and every push of the pedal, you can start to think about what other parts of the bike are doing, as well as the effects of your developing cycling skills on the way in which the bike behaves. It is much like this in the classroom, you begin to be aware of the impact of your teaching on pupils' learning and behaviour. Like pushing the pedals, you don't need to think about everything you do in the classroom, some teaching skills become more routine. This routinization is important, and when you reach this stage, you are more than just surviving, you are now *coping*. As we saw in Chapter 4, Cathryn reached this stage by the end of her first term in teaching.

↓

'Once you can ride well, you start looking around and seeing what's going on around you'. Similarly in the classroom, as you acquire more teaching skills and more of these skills become automatic, you find you can do more *exploring*. Abbey was in her second year when she reached the exploring stage. As she explained, *'The planning's a lot easier, I feel I can put a bit of imagination into it now, rather than just existing with it'*.

↓

And when you get really good, you can try out wheelies and even practise riding without holding the handlebars. You become more *proficient*, but you do also need to beware in case you fall off! As we saw in Chapter 4, both Abbey and Cathryn were proceeding with suitable caution at this stage.

↓

Developing Professional Learning

Figure 8.2 From beginning primary teaching to developing professional learning

Although Activity 8.1 and Figure 8.2 focus on Abbey's and Cathryn's general stages of development, neither teacher acquired teaching skills uniformly across all subjects. In our research we found that most of the newly qualified teachers entered the profession at a coping stage in relation to the core subjects (especially numeracy and literacy), and at a survival stage in relation to the non-core subjects. In addition, within each stage there was a range of levels of competence, for instance within the 'surviving' stage the levels ranged from barely surviving to surviving well. Similarly with the other stages there was a range of levels of competence (see Figure 8.3). The development of the new teachers' subject expertise during their first year of teaching was interesting, as most of the new teachers said that they developed further in the core subjects than in the non-core subjects. This was partly because they were already confident in these areas, and partly because systems and resources supporting these subjects were well established in schools. For example, one teacher said, 'I've been able to observe others and because you teach them [the core subjects] regularly, my skills have developed'. Many of the teachers also talked about subject coordinators in schools who helped them extend their practice. By the end of their first year in teaching many new teachers had moved to an exploratory stage for literacy and numeracy (see Figure 8.3).

On the other hand, in relation to teaching the non-core subjects many new teachers felt they had made limited progress during their NQT year. In some subjects in particular many new teachers felt they were at the coping or even still at the survival stage in terms of their teaching skills (see Figure 8.3). This was often in spite of having been on in-service courses, and was usually because there was less emphasis in the school on these subjects than, for instance, on mathematics and English. For example, one teacher cited music as the area in which she had made the least progress during the first year, explaining that: 'I've tried to avoid teaching it as I have little knowledge and experience of it'. She was able to do this because a music specialist came into school to teach the subject, an often cited situation. As we saw in Chapter 5, lack of guidance, lack of time spent on some subjects of the curriculum or inadequate resources were reasons frequently mentioned, particularly in relation to subjects such as music, PE, design and technology and art. As a result many newly qualified teachers to whom we spoke felt that the relative lack of preparedness for teaching non-core subjects in initial training, coupled with the lack of emphasis on these subjects in schools, had led to a widening of their relative levels of competence across the range of primary school subjects during their first year(s) of teaching. The gap between their teaching skills in some core and non-core subjects had tended to grow with, at one end, the non-core subject in which they had made least progress (such as music in the case of the teacher mentioned above) and, at the other end, the core subject(s) in which they felt they had made most progress (see Figure 8.3).

The next section of this chapter moves on from discussing the acquisition of teaching skills to considering other professional demands placed on teachers but, before you read this, have a go at Activity 8.2. This activity considers what happened to Abbey and Cathryn, but this time it focuses on how they managed the professional demands of their new posts.

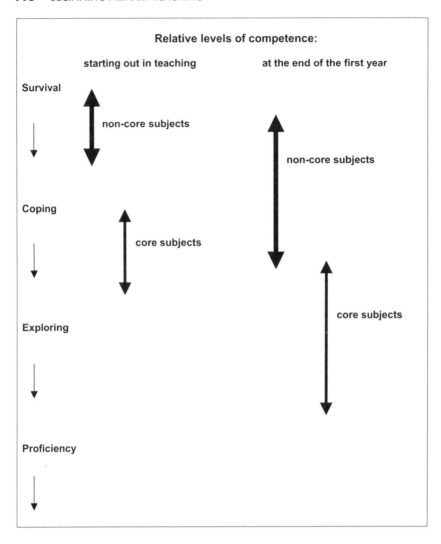

Figure 8.3   The acquisition of teaching skills when starting out in teaching and at the end of the first year

Activity 8.2

Think about your response to Activity 8.1 where you identified when Abbey and Cathryn reached each of the four stages: survival, coping, exploring and proficiency.

Some of the factors which affected Abbey's and Cathryn's development as teachers were to do with the acquisition of teaching skills. But not all were. Make a list of all the other professional demands they faced and what contributed to the two teachers' professional development in these areas. You may need to re-read the first section of Chapter 4 (this section is called: 'What happened to the four teachers in their first three years?') to remind you of how they developed.

Other professional demands

The acquisition of teaching skills is clearly important, but this is only part of the picture. As we saw in the earlier chapters of this book, the ability to cope with other professional demands was also crucial for Abbey, Cathryn, Fatou, Gina and the other new teachers. When we analysed data from our research, four stages emerged in the teachers' ability to cope with these professional demands. The first two stages were the same as for the acquisition of teaching skills: survival and coping. The third and fourth stages were realism and balance (see Figure 8.4).

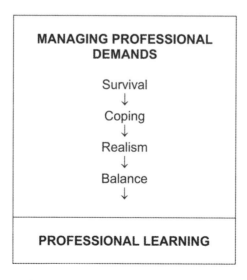

Figure 8.4   Stages in the ability to manage professional demands

There were some areas of teaching where new teachers had felt less well prepared by their initial training, for example classroom management and working with children with special needs. In addition, there were some wider aspects of their teaching role, such as dealing with parents, in which they also felt less well prepared. However, by the end of their first year most new teachers felt they had made significant progress in their ability to manage these broader professional demands. Although they had started at a survival stage and had found these areas particularly challenging, most teachers had gained confidence and were more than coping with the professional demands by the end of the year. This was largely because they had gained plenty of experience in these areas throughout the year. Increased experience had occurred mainly through necessity: these were now essential aspects of the job and there was no class teacher or mentor to take over the responsibility for any of these areas. In terms of other professional demands, such as planning and assessment, most new teachers had already felt well prepared by their initial training; however, once teaching full-time in school they realized that although their training had prepared them to plan for lessons, it had not prepared them for teaching the entire primary curriculum on a long-term basis. Planning with long-term goals in mind and for all aspects of the primary curriculum was a way of working that the new teachers had to adjust to. However, generally the teachers considered that they had made progress in terms of planning in their first year of teaching, largely because of the structures in place in schools and the opportunity to work alongside experienced teachers.

By the end of their first year in teaching, new teachers tended to have reached a coping stage in relation to wider professional demands and their overall workload. Some were beginning to reduce their working hours outside the school day and most were moving towards a more realistic appraisal of what they could manage in order to maintain a life outside teaching. But not all were. For a number of reasons, some new teachers were still at a survival stage when it came to dealing with the professional demands placed on them.

When we talked to new teachers early in their second year of teaching, they described in a range of ways how they were managing to deal with the demands of teaching. These first two quotes were from teachers who were still very much at a *survival* stage:

> There's still so much to do, and although I've got the same year group again, Years 4 and 5, this group is so different to the other group, they're so bright, so there's an awful lot of planning for me to do now, so I'm still working long hours.

> I suppose it is just the organization, I still feel like a headless chicken sometimes. There's still so much to do and I'm still marking 'til really

late. I'd like to feel I was better organized and able to get through the work more quickly.

Being like a 'headless chicken' and working long hours were key characteristics of the survival stage. The next two teachers had moved beyond survival and were now generally *coping* with professional demands. When talking about whether or not they found things easier as they started out in their second year of teaching, they said:

> It's about the same really, I'm just learning to organize myself better, so that makes things easier.

> [My workload] has reduced since last year. There is still an awful lot to do, but I feel a bit more on top of it, I feel more able to manage now.

The next two teachers had moved beyond a coping stage, to *realism*:

> I don't do detailed lesson plans and I usually stay longer on a Friday now, to sort myself out for the next week, so I don't work at the weekends now, I just do a little bit on a Sunday sometimes.

> I've reduced the amount of planning I was doing, because I decided that it wouldn't reduce the quality of the lessons and so I'm finding the planning a lot easier and finding I need to do a lot less. It's still detailed and it's still there, but I'm just spending less time on it.

Key characteristics of the realism stage were an ability to manage time more effectively, not simply by doing less, but by a more realistic appraisal of where energies needed to be targeted. Generally this came with a better understanding of themselves as teachers and an increased knowledge of where their strengths and weaknesses lay, but also as a result of some skills becoming semi-routinized: for instance, not everything now needed to be planned in an overly long and detailed manner.

> Yes, [my workload] has reduced. I don't do as much in the evenings now. I maybe do half an hour or an hour at the most because some of the things are repetitive and I have already done them. I also don't work on Sundays now. I felt I wasn't coping with that, working all week and then Sundays as well, it didn't suit me, so I have weekends free now and it's better for me to have a complete break. What I do now is work for long hours on Thursday night, I do all the planning on Thursday for the following week. It does mean that on a Thursday

night I think, 'Oh no, I've got a lot of work ahead of me'. But it's worth it because then at the weekend, I know I have a clear weekend and I prefer it that way.

Evidence of teachers having achieved *balance* was rare early in the second year of teaching, although some teachers (as this last quote illustrates) were aware that they would need to achieve this. Figure 8.5 illustrates how Abbey and Cathryn moved through these four stages during their first years of teaching. You may find it helpful to refer back to what you did in Activities 8.1 and 8.2, or re-read their stories in the first section of Chapter 4 before referring to Figure 8.5.

Apart from factors already mentioned, other key aspects which appeared to help new teachers to become realistic, regardless of age and training route, were prior work experience and whether they had children of their own. Where teachers had prior experience of working in the classroom, for example as a parent helper or as a teaching assistant, they tended to be more realistic about the standards they set for themselves to achieve and about the time they could give to aspects of their work such as planning and preparation. Also, where the new teachers had children of their own, this tended to result in them being realistic about the amount of time they could spend on work outside of the classroom as they had relatively heavy demands on their time placed on them by their families. This sense of being realistic in terms of managing professional demands was even more evident when looking at the cohort group in their third year of teaching, many of whom had reached the stage of balance. For example, one teacher advised new teachers as follows:

> What you've got to do is to try to be realistic about what you're going to achieve. It's good enough to be a good teacher with a bit of brilliance but don't expect to be brilliant all the time ... There is life outside school.

By the third year, some teachers who had not reached a stage of balance were considering leaving the profession as they often felt unable to successfully manage the demands of teaching.

A model of professional development and learning

The previous two sections of this chapter have looked at the acquisition of teaching skills and also the development of teachers' ability to cope with professional demands. However, these two aspects of professional learning do not develop separately, they are closely interrelated. When explaining the

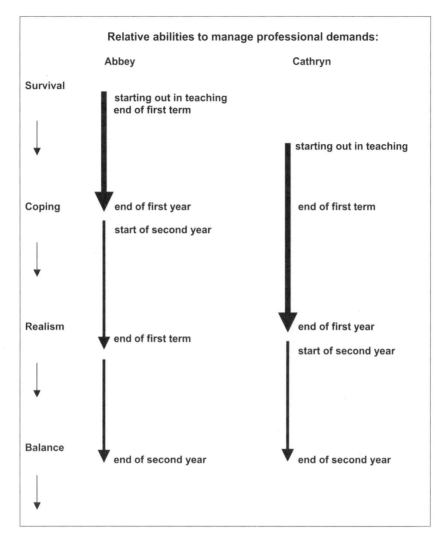

Figure 8.5 The ability to manage professional demands in the early years of teaching: Abbey and Cathryn

aspects of school life in which they felt they had developed most, during their second year of teaching, two teachers said:

> That's definitely dealing with parents, I feel far more confident about that now. At first I was really nervous with parents, I didn't know what to say, but now, I suppose because also I'm in my second year, they treat me as a teacher rather than an NQT and I am far more

confident. And also the general day to day organization and running of the class. I've tried things now, and I know what works and what doesn't work, so I've certainly developed in my classroom organization, I'm far more confident about it.

Definitely time management. I've learned how to manage my time better so I don't spend quite so long now on things. I do more marking in lessons now and I save time on my planning, but now I've taken on a new year group and the PE coordinator's role. I'm still spending a lot of time planning and working so I suppose the workload had reduced by the end of last year, but it's gone back up again now.

In both these examples, the teacher's acquisition of teaching skills and their ability to cope with professional demands are clearly interlinked. In the first example, the teacher's skills in the classroom and knowing 'what works and what doesn't work' had helped raise the teacher's confidence level and their ability to deal with the wider professional demands of teaching. In the second example, the teacher was faced with learning new teaching skills as PE coordinator in the second year of teaching, which led to an increased workload for a while with the additional planning this involved. Figure 8.6 depicts this relationship between acquisition of teaching skills and the ability to cope with professional demands. The arrows looping upwards depict how, at times, we may return to an earlier stage, for instance when we take on additional responsibilities or change school or class (as with the quote by the PE coordinator above).

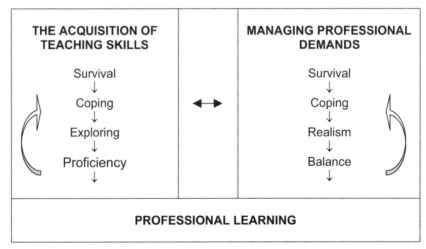

Figure 8.6 A model of professional learning, linking acquisition of teaching skills with the ability to manage professional demands

The model presented here emerged through our research with the new teachers and our analysis of what they said to us about their experiences during the early years of their new career. However, our reading of some theoretical and research-based work also influenced our thinking. In developing our model, we adapted the stages of development which have been identified during initial teacher training (e.g. Calderhead 1988; Tomlinson 1995) and thought about them in relation to the first years of teaching. What we found out from the new teachers about their learning and support during initial training was also fed into the development of the model. The last section of this chapter introduces and discusses the notion of 'stages' in the development of professional learning and brings a note of caution to how stages may be used.

Stages of development in professional learning

The idea of stages of development in beginning teaching is not new, although most developmental models tend to apply to initial teacher training rather than to the early years of teaching (e.g. Furlong and Maynard 1995). Berliner (1987) identified five stages of teacher development from novice to expert, which are very similar to the Dreyfus model of professional development (Dreyfus and Dreyfus 1986). The problem with stages is however, as Calderhead and Shorrock (1997) argue, that stages of development can be an over-simplification: beginning teachers do not always progress in the linear fashion implied by a developmental model. Nevertheless, Calderhead and Shorrock's (1997) case studies do indicate a certain progression from survival to coping in the first term(s) of teaching, something which we also found in our research with new teachers. The model of early professional development presented in this chapter moves away from one that is strictly linear: it separates teaching skills from other professional demands, and allows for progression at different rates within different areas while acknowledging and highlighting their interrelationship. However, as Eraut (1994) argues, the nature of the links between stages and areas of development is not straightforward and we will return to this in Chapter 9.

One aspect of the model which it is important to highlight at this point, and which was identified earlier in the chapter, is that of routinization. In other words, some skills become more routine, and then tend not to be thought through and thought about in as great a depth as previously. Routinization reduces cognitive load and knowledge comes tacit. By this we mean that as some skills become more routine in the classroom we don't think in quite the same way as previously, in other words, we think less in 'long-hand' and think more in 'short-hand'. An example of this would be getting the class to clear away quickly and efficiently at the end of a messy activity. Skilled teachers have the classroom, the activity and the children organized in such a way that this can seem to happen like magic, maximizing the teaching and learning time in the lesson. However, beginning teachers have to think through carefully (in 'long-hand') how this will happen, where to place materials, who will do what and when, how long it will take, etc. All this takes a lot of time and energy.

The point here in relation to the stages of the model, is that unless there is some routinization, cognitive overload occurs and we get the 'headless chicken' scenario. Thinking in 'short-hand' helps us move beyond survival and helps us cope with the complexities of teaching and learning, not just with some of the classroom routines (such as clearing away). But, does routinization mean that we can stop thinking in detail about some aspects of our work? Do these aspects become taken for granted and if so, does it matter? For instance with the clearing away activity, who does which jobs and does this matter? We will return to this in Chapter 9 as we look more critically at professional development.

More recently, discussions in the literature concerning professional knowledge and learning have surrounded ideas about the speed at which professionals work when engaged in professional tasks, and the thinking which goes on as they work (e.g. Eraut 2004). We know that as professional knowledge becomes tacit it also becomes more difficult for professionals to explain what they do. What thinking does go on? What does it mean to be thinking in 'short-hand'? It is likely that you experienced this kind of situation when you were training: sometimes if a trainee asks their mentor in school to explain what they just did in the classroom, the mentor has to stop and think about it, as it can be something that they will tell you that they 'just did'.

Different from the above, there has been a focus in some studies on identifying stages in teachers' careers within a more holistic context, for instance looking at teachers' personal as well as professional lives (e.g. Levinson 1978; Sikes et al. 1985; Goodson 1992; Huberman 1993). These studies also have a developmental component which had relevance for our model, particularly the early career phases. For example, Sikes et al. (1985), drawing on Levinson's model (1978), describe an initial phase in terms of survival and 'reality shock' (relating to the first years of teaching), with phase two (after six to seven years in teaching) characterized by feelings of competence accompanied, for some, by a questioning of their career choice and direction. Our research with new teachers in their first few years of teaching indicates that these phases seem to be coming earlier (for example, after two to three years) and are perhaps more condensed. Despite the questions which still surround stages of development (e.g. Eraut 1994, 2004), the stages in our model have proved useful in both describing and explaining what was happening in relation to the professional development and learning of beginning teachers.

However, it is important not to treat the stages as rigid categories, but as indicative categories and as a way of thinking about development.

Key findings and action points

This chapter has introduced a model of professional learning which inter-relates two key aspects:

- the acquisition of teaching skills and
- the ability to manage professional demands.

We found that teachers tended to pass through four main stages as their teaching skills developed in the early years of their careers: survival, coping, exploring and proficiency. However, the acquisition of teaching skills was often not uniform across all subjects and aspects of teaching for a number of reasons. New teachers found that they tended to improve, unsurprisingly, in areas in which they had had most experience and where they received support and help from more experienced teachers.

Of equal importance to the development of professional learning was the ability to manage professional demands and we found that teachers tended to pass through the following stages: survival, coping, realism and balance. What emerged as of particular significance was the need to be aware of this aspect of professional development and learning, as well as the need to achieve realism and balance. The acquisition of teaching skills is important, but it is not the whole picture.

Action points

- Expect a steep learning curve in your first year of teaching.
- You can't do everything at once, so try to pace yourself.
- However, at the same time be aware of any areas of professional development which you may be avoiding (like the example given in this chapter where some new teachers avoided teaching music).
- Seek help from colleagues in school and work on developing effective relationships with these colleagues – never underestimate the importance of this.

Concluding discussion

Professional learning and development are complex and involve the interrelationship of the acquisition of teaching skills and the ability to manage professional demands. Although clearly one is no good without the other, we found that sometimes the ability to manage professional demands was underestimated. We also found that some new teachers were working extremely long hours, sometimes every evening as well as long hours at the weekend, just to keep their heads above water. Sometimes this was something they kept quiet about in school.

Teachers need to achieve a work–life balance and learn to do so without compromising standards and quality in teaching. Like learning to ride a bike, some skills become more routine as new teachers become more experienced, and it is important that this happens if a work–life balance is to be achieved. Although it is tricky, the majority of beginning teachers did manage to achieve a more balanced approach by the end of their second or third year. Those that didn't achieve balance by their third year were often thinking about leaving the profession.

If you experience difficulties early in your career, or simply find you are getting over-tired, take a step back and think about two things:

1   Just how far you have developed professionally since your initial teacher training (remember that steep learning curve!).
2   Ask yourself where the problems lie and remember both sides of the model.

We will discuss this further in the next chapter where we will be reflecting more on the model and using it as a way of helping you understand yourself more as a teacher.

Further reading and useful website links

Bubb, S. and Earley, P. (2004) *Managing Teacher Workload*. London: Paul Chapman.
Eraut, M. (1994) *Developing Professional Knowledge and Competence*. London: Falmer Press.
Pollard, A. (2002a) *Reflective Teaching: Effective and Evidence-informed Professional Practice*. London: Continuum.
Pollard, A. (2002b) *Readings for Reflective Teaching*. London: Continuum.

9

Understanding yourself as a teacher

This chapter follows on from the last by asking the reader to locate themselves in the model and thus help them to identify and reflect on areas of strength and further development. However, understanding yourself as a teacher involves more than this: the chapter moves on to suggest practical ways of improving practice in an action-oriented way. Action research, professional development and school improvement are all considered.

Introduction

In the last chapter we introduced you to a model of professional development which helps us understand the ways in which new teachers tend to develop in their first years of teaching. We focused on the professional development of Abbey and Cathryn and saw from their experiences that rates of professional development can vary, for a number of reasons. Although their rates of progress and professional development differed, by the end of their second year in teaching, both new teachers had reached roughly the same point in relation to their ability to manage professional demands (see Figure 8.5).

When we focused on the acquisition of teaching skills, we saw that there tended to be a range of rates of progress in relation to levels of competence among new teachers in their first two years of teaching (see Figure 8.3) often related to the core and non-core subjects and the experiences and support new teachers had had during their first year(s) in teaching. Not all teachers developed professionally in a smooth, progressive manner. In this chapter we will focus on Fatou's and Gina's experiences and start to explore what happened to them during their early teaching career. In addition, we will look at ways in which you can begin to think about your stage of development and what you can do to improve your practice in schools.

What happened to Fatou and Gina?

We will start this section with a task, Activity 9.1, which aims to focus on what happened to Fatou and Gina, as well as to begin to identify their patterns of professional development.

Activity 9.1

Turn back to the first section of Chapter 4 and read Fatou's and Gina's stories again. The section is entitled: 'What happened to the four teachers in their first three years?' Now look at Figure 9.1 which shows their patterns of development during their first years of teaching.

Focus on Fatou's professional learning during her first year in teaching (as illustrated in Figure 9.1). Within the 'Acquisition of Teaching Skills' column you will see that Fatou moved from 'coping' at the beginning of her first year to 'exploring' by the end of the year. Using the information given in Chapter 4, what evidence is there to demonstrate this?

When you have done this, see if you can do the same for Fatou's second and third years in teaching.

Fatou's and Gina's experiences in teaching highlight a number of important issues, including:

- *Teaching is a complex career and teachers develop professionally at different rates and for different reasons.* The four new teachers featured in this book all had different patterns of development, but these were not the only patterns we encountered. The difference is perhaps clearest if we compare, year by year, Fatou's and Gina's ability to manage professional demands (see Figure 9.1). Although they finish roughly at the same stage after four years in teaching, their pathways were very different for different reasons (as we saw in Part 1 of this book).

- *When we change contexts or jobs, or take on new challenges or responsibilities, we can find ourselves moving back to earlier stages in the model.* This is quite normal and can happen to anyone at any stage of their career. For example, Fatou progressed quickly through the early stages during her first two years in teaching in relation both to the acquisition of teaching skills and the ability to manage professional demands. This could be explained mainly because of her familiarity and extended experiences with the same year group within the same school. However this did mean that her experiences were more

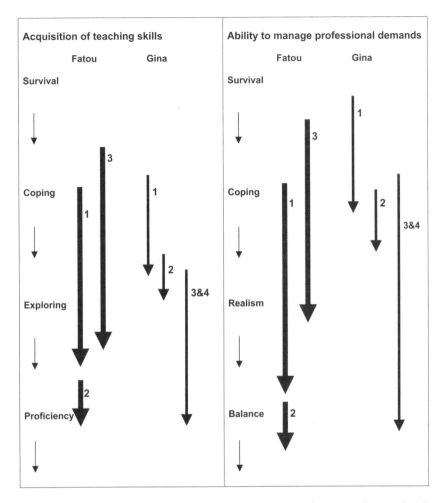

Key: The numbers represent years 1–3 in teaching in Fatou's case and years 1–4 in Gina's

Figure 9.1   Professional learning: Fatou and Gina

restricted than the other three teachers' and she then seemed to take a step backwards at the start of her third year in teaching. However, her teaching skills had not really gone backwards, she was now adding to her professional development. Although she found the transfer of learning challenging from one context to another and from one year group to another, she did succeed in doing it.

- *It is important to know and understand yourself as a teacher.* Gina for instance, changed to a part-time teaching job because she wanted to continue teaching, but found it difficult to balance the demands of home and school when working full-time. She was aware that it wasn't her teaching skills that were the problem but her ability to cope with the other professional demands while also balancing the demands of her family and personal life.

The next section builds on this last point by asking you to consider your own professional development.

Locating yourself in the model

We have spent some time looking at the model in relation to the four new teachers, but now it is your turn. In this section, we will start with a task which will help you to locate yourself in the model and also help you to identify and reflect on your areas of strength and areas for further development. To do this next task you will need copies of the blank chart (Figure 9.2). You may also find it useful to go back to Figure 8.2 which used the analogy of riding a bike, and re-read the descriptions of stages in the acquisition of teaching skills.

Activity 9.2

We will begin by focusing just on the acquisition of teaching skills. Start by thinking about the primary school subject you feel most confident teaching. Using the descriptions in Figure 8.2, which stage would you put yourself in at this point in time: survival, coping, exploring or proficiency? Once you have decided on the stage which is most appropriate for yourself, decide where in that stage you are. Do you think you are just into that stage, or maybe well into that stage? Mark this on Figure 9.2, the professional learning chart.

Now think back to a year ago. Where would you have put yourself then? Again, mark this on the chart. If there has been a change, which is highly likely, can you explain what has brought about the change?

Now choose a subject in which you feel less confident and go through the same process, plotting on the chart your stages of development in relation to the model. Compare your rates of progress over the year with the two subjects. Also compare which stages you passed through in relation to each of the subjects.

Once you have completed Activity 9.2 you can repeat the process for:

- specific subjects or areas of the curriculum;
- other aspects of teaching (such as classroom management or taking assemblies);

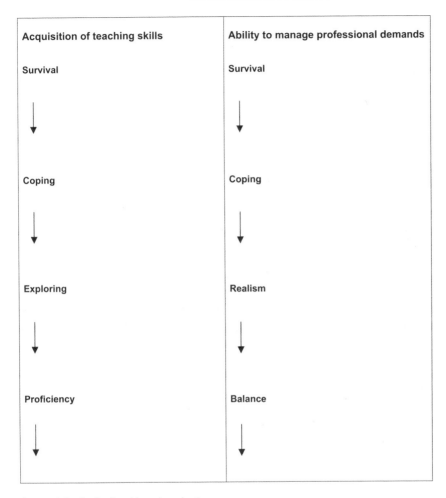

Figure 9.2 Professional learning chart

- particular years or terms in teaching (for example, compare your first term in teaching with where you are now);
- different teaching contexts (for instance before or after a change of class, year group or school).

Identifying and reflecting on stages of development, in relation to acquiring the skills of teaching, may help you to identify and reflect on where you need to put your energies and also help you know yourself better as a teacher. However, as we pointed out in the last chapter, the acquisition of teaching skills is only part of the picture. You now also need to focus on how you are managing all the additional professional demands of teaching. Be strict with yourself on this too. Think carefully before you begin to plot your professional development on the model. As above, you can focus on particular professional demands (such as planning, managing paperwork or perhaps working with parents). You could also focus on specific contexts or groups of children or how you have developed over a period of time. The important thing is to make the process of plotting yourself on the model work for you. Use it to help you reflect on your professional learning and help you to understand yourself better.

Reflecting on your professional development

So now you know where you are in terms of your professional development, but where are you going next? What do you think you need to focus on in order to develop further professionally? What are your short and your longer term goals? In this section, we will focus more specifically on practical ways in which you can improve your practice.

You are likely to have heard the term 'reflective practitioner' a number of times before. Pollard provides an informative overview of reflective teaching in which he highlights that: 'Newly Qualified Teachers may use reflection as a means of self-consciously increasing understanding and capability' (2002a: 12). In this section we will focus on reflection and reflective practice but also ask you to think more about how your own practice is developing and how you might support this process in an action-oriented way. Reflective action, as Pollard points out: 'involves a willingness to engage in constant self-appraisal and development' (2002a: 12).

Many new teachers to whom we spoke identified the shock factor when they first started their new job, often describing it in the following way:

> It's a tough job, you don't switch off. If you're dedicated you take the children's problems home. You're their social worker, their mum, everything, but no one tells you that before you start, even on teaching practice, you don't take on those roles, so it's a bit of a shock when you start.

The beginning teacher above and many others described in similar ways how they were frequently taking problems home with them (the children's problems and their own). They often described how reflections on their practice tended to be mainly after the end of the day (often in the evening) and were often wrapped up with concerns for the children in their class, especially concerns with children they had difficulty managing or providing for academically. The question they most frequently found themselves asking was, 'What shall I do about . . . ?' This kind of reflection tended to change gradually as they moved from survival to the coping stage and then on to the exploring or realism stages of the model. As this happened, the questions tended to change to: 'What effect will it have if I do this?', or, 'What if I don't do that?' For instance, if I change the way I introduce the lesson, or try a particular behaviour strategy, or don't respond to the children who shout out. Increasingly reflection tended to become more concerned with immediate action and interaction in the classroom situation and what the teacher could do to improve this. This could take the form of what Schon (1983) calls 'reflection-in-action' (i.e. as it happens) which new teachers find quite difficult, or 'reflection-on-action' (i.e. reflection soon after the event). Both are important.

At the end of their first year, the teacher quoted above talked in the following way about aspects of school life in which they felt they had made the least progress:

> I think organizing my time and prioritizing. I didn't seem to have time for anything. I spent so much time on school work so I've got to learn to organize my time better ... I realize every day is different but I know where to cut corners now, I'm learning that. Last year I kind of got by delivering lessons, it was all new. But now this year what I want to do is make the lessons more interesting, evaluate the lessons more, evaluate what I'm doing so I can change things that aren't right.

What do you think this teacher meant by the last sentence? What was meant by saying 'what I want to do is ... evaluate the lessons more, evaluate what I'm doing so I can change things that aren't right'? Wasn't this already happening? Lesson evaluation is part of what you do right from when you begin your initial teacher training, but what early career teachers often found was that they spent more time rather than less time evaluating and reflecting on their practice as they went through their first years of teaching. As teachers became more experienced, and moved into the exploring stages of teaching they became more able to engage in reflection-in-action as well as continuing to develop reflection-on-action. This was not always formal written evaluation or reflection. A different but related skill which some teachers developed as they grew more proficient was the ability to ask more searching questions. How can you address these issues and questions in relation to your own teaching? The next section offers some practical suggestions for improving your practice.

Using research to develop your practice

There are a number of ways in which you can engage in examining your own practice in a more systematic and rigorous manner. You will hear people talk about 'action research', 'practitioner research' or 'teacher research'. Increasingly teachers are carrying out small-scale projects in their own classroom, sometimes with the support of, or collaboratively with, colleagues.

The important thing to remember is that you don't need to go for anything grand or large-scale to be effective. In fact, it is just the opposite. If you want to develop your practice, you should think small and focus on the small things about your practice that you would like to change. Asking the 'what if … ?' questions can be really worthwhile (for example, 'What if I change the way in which I group the children for numeracy?' or, 'What if I ask more questions of the children when I introduce the art topic, rather than giving them instructions?' or even, 'What if I decide just to wait for silence before I let them go out to play, instead of repeatedly asking them to be quiet, before they are allowed out?')

You can make use of some research techniques to help you to answer or address your questions, and we will use two real examples of research that early career teachers have undertaken in order to show you how this can be done.

Example 1: How can I improve my teaching in literacy lessons?

This was a question one teacher initially asked of their own practice. However, the question quickly changed as they started to think more about it and realized that there was another question that needed to be asked first: 'What is my teaching like in a literacy lesson?' In order to improve our teaching we first need to try to understand what is actually happening in the classroom.

Having realized this, other questions came tumbling out: 'What do I actually do during the lesson? What do the children do? What kind of questions do I ask? What kind of questions do the children ask?' and so on. The teacher quickly realized that there were lots of questions about their current practices that needed to be asked, so what should they do to try to answer these questions?

The approach this teacher used was to tape record a lesson. The first decision was not to do anything different, just to plan as usual, organize and teach as usual, but also to record the lesson from start to finish. As there was a teaching assistant in the room for that lesson, the teacher also asked the teaching assistant to do two things: first to make a list of which children spoke and who put their hand up whenever the teacher was addressing the class as a whole (this would make the tape recording easier to analyse);

secondly, when group work was going on, to track the teacher's movements by marking these movements on a plan of the classroom. The teaching assistant had a few goes at trying out the recording before they decided to do it for real. Although the teacher was initially self-conscious about being recorded and was worried that this may affect the way they taught, in reality the tape recorder was quickly forgotten. The teacher said that the advantage of this method was that they were the only person who would need to listen to the tape – there were no observers (apart from the teaching assistant who was always in there anyway).

But was this OK? Should the children and their parents know that they are being recorded? For what purpose? Should the headteacher know what is planned? The teacher realized that these and other similar ethical questions needed to be considered, so before going ahead with the recording the teacher checked them out with the headteacher. Once all was agreed they were off.

After the lesson, the teacher found there was a lot of data to analyse: the taped lesson, the two records the teaching assistant had made, the children's work and the lesson plans. However, the teachers also decided one more thing was needed, that was to ask the children what they thought they had learnt in that lesson. This was done as soon as the pupils came in from play and they all wrote a short response to the question.

So what did the teacher find out? Far more than anticipated, including:

- The teacher did far more talking than they thought they had done.
- Some children had put up their hand many times, but had never been chosen to respond to a question.
- Questions tended to go to those children sitting centrally. The teacher realized that those children sitting on the outer edges of the class group tended to be forgotten.
- Questions tended to be more closed than open (i.e. requiring short or one word answers) and were often more to 'test' children, rather than provoke thinking and discussion.
- When group work was going on, the teacher found far more time was spent going backwards and forwards to one particular group than they had been aware of doing.
- There were also some surprises with individual children: for example, one child who generally appeared to take little part in literacy lessons demonstrated a surprisingly good understanding of the main learning intention of the lesson.

But perhaps the biggest surprise this teacher had came from the children's responses when asked what they had learnt from the lesson. Although pleased that, generally, what they thought they had learnt matched what the teacher thought was being taught, a surprising number of other 'things learnt' were listed. For instance, one pupil thought they had mainly learnt about 'how to draw', whereas this had been the mode of recording chosen by that particular pupil as part of one short exercise within the lesson.

This analysis provided the teacher with a very wide range of things to follow up and led to a number of new questions. It also prompted the teacher to reflect more carefully on what they were doing in the classroom. The teacher began to ask more searching questions of some aspects of their work that they realized had become part of their routine practice (such as asking questions more to those sitting centrally in the room).

Example 2: Consulting pupils about their learning

This second example extends one of the methods used in the previous ex-ample. It was almost as an after-thought that the teacher in Example 1 decided to ask the children what they thought they had learnt from the lesson. Although the teacher learnt a tremendous amount from the other methods used, this single short activity proved to be more powerful than anticipated.

In this second example, the teacher decided to consult the pupils about their learning. The decision to do this stemmed from some work carried out with the class on learning styles and how to identify their preferred learning styles. This made the teacher think more about the pupils' learning as well as their own teaching. What was the connection? The teacher had come to realize that teaching something didn't automatically mean that the children learnt it.

The teacher started with a task similar to the task in Example 1 above. At the end of a lesson, the children were asked to note down what they had learnt in that lesson. The teacher then compared the pupils' responses with what had been planned. The teacher also reflected back over the lesson itself and made notes about what might have influenced what the pupils felt they had learnt. This proved to be as revealing for this teacher as it was for the teacher in the first example, so the exercise was repeated the next day having first made some changes to both the planning and the delivery of the next lesson. This process was repeated several times, and before long the teacher realized that the pupils were anticipating this request and were thinking more within the lesson itself about what was being taught. They also began to ask questions in class about what they were learning.

As a result of this small task, this teacher explained how a small but fundamental change was made to their teaching. The learning objectives of the lesson were now made far more explicit – both to the teacher and to the children. Having reflected critically on what they had been doing in the planning and the delivery, the teacher found that they themselves had sometimes not really been clear about the main learning objectives of the lesson. In fact the teacher decided that sometimes these had been 'at best, woolly'. This would now change.

Also as a result of the effectiveness of this task, the teacher decided to consult the pupils on a more regular basis about their learning. The Year 6 class were given research journals in which they recorded thoughts in response to specific questions. The kinds of questions they were asked were, for example:

- What part of the lesson did you enjoy most?
- Why was this?
- In which part of the lesson did you learn most? Why?
- What prevents you from learning?

The journals were used for about ten minutes once a week at the end of specific lessons and proved to be as revealing about both learning and teaching as the earlier exercise the teacher had used.

Once you have tried this approach, you may find it is as effective as these two teachers found. You may also find that you enjoy the process and you want to go on and do more research. Many teachers do. You will certainly find that it can help your acquisition of teaching skills and your ability to manage professional demands if you focus your questions and reflections on the small-scale things about your practice that you would like to change or that you would like to understand better. Don't forget the 'what if ... ?' questions; these help us question the effects of some of our more routine practices.

The next section in this chapter discusses some of the findings from our research with new teachers focusing on the main factors which influenced professional learning in the early years of primary teaching. It is likely that you will be able to identify from this some of the factors that have influenced or are influencing your own development.

Professional learning and the acquisition of professional knowledge

As we have seen in this and the previous chapter, professional learning is complex. It can be characterized not only in terms of skill development, such as how to handle a class or how to teach a subject, but also by a developing understanding of wider professional roles and responsibilities (Hargreaves and Fullan 1992; Calderhead and Shorrock 1997). A similar distinction underpins the model presented in this book in which teachers' learning is not only demonstrated through growing capability in the classroom but also through the ability to cope with broader professional demands, such as managing paperwork and relationships with parents.

The process of acquiring professional knowledge is, as Eraut (2002b) argues, highly complex and individual. It involves the interaction between personal experience and a series of situations within particular contexts. There are a number of factors which affect professional learning and the acquisition of professional knowledge. We found that one of the key factors was the existence of *support* (although this was not unproblematic, i.e. not all support was effective support). Another was the *culture of the school* itself (some schools were more supportive of new teachers than others). The two key factors of support and the culture of the school are discussed in more detail below.

Types and levels of support

We identified a number of different types of support which beginning teachers identified as important to their professional development. Feedback from colleagues, mentors, senior managers in school (e.g. headteachers or year leaders), parents and pupils themselves were all important. We saw for instance that Cathryn gained in confidence after positive feedback from Ofsted during their school's inspection. Another type of support which new teachers found valuable came through activities where they worked jointly with colleagues, as in Cathryn's case where she jointly planned with her mentor during her first year of teaching. Similarly other learning opportunities could provide valuable support to new teachers, for instance observing another colleague at work, or having the opportunity to visit another school or class.

Building on work by Yeomans and Sampson (1994), we were able to identify three broad levels of support which were important to the early development of newly qualified primary teachers:

1 *Personal*: more informal support provided by colleagues and friends, both in and out of school.
2 *Professional*: leadership provided by the headteacher, working alongside experienced teachers and team teaching.
3 *Structural*: systems and procedures in place in school and in the local education authority.

The teachers in our research studies identified supportive relationships with colleagues as being of particular importance in their professional learning, followed closely by support from school management. These issues have been noted by others, for instance Sturman (2003) in relation to relationships in the primary context and Blandford (2000) who identified a range of formal mechanisms of professional support. In our research we also found that where support from management was lacking, professional development of new teachers could be significantly impeded, which could in turn affect retention (a factor also noted by Craft 2000 and Sturman 2003). Central to the success of support for new teachers seemed to be the relationships that were developed. In some cases support from management was indirect, worked through the development and sustenance of a supportive culture and a learning climate.

The culture of the school

The culture of a school can exert a strong influence on the professional development of new teachers. When reporting on successful primary schools, Ofsted (2002) identified the importance of strong leadership and vision in establishing a creative and effective learning community. In addition, Eraut (2002a) has argued that such a community is characterized by 'positive relationships of mutual respect and the positive recognition and expectation of mutual learning' (p. 178). The importance of relationships as highlighted by Eraut has also been highlighted by others (e.g. Ofsted 2002; Sturman 2003; Fielding et al. 2005) and it is not hard to imagine that if a new teacher starts their career in a school which has such an effective learning community, that new teacher is likely to have many of the right conditions for positive professional development. We saw some examples of this in Chapter 7.

Within creative and effective organizational cultures there are structures and practices which have been shown to enable and promote professional learning for all teachers (Zeichner et al. 1987). For example, Ofsted (2002) identified efficient approaches to planning including using ICT, which released more time for teaching. At the level of practice, Craft (2000) and Blandford (2000) have both highlighted opportunities for professional learning such as peer tutoring, coaching by a colleague with particular expertise, paired observation, team teaching and mentoring. As we have seen in earlier chapters, the new teachers to whom we spoke also noted these factors as particularly important for them too.

These kinds of organizational factors can exert such a strong influence upon the new teacher that they may even 'dominate and overrule the practices learned in college' (Calderhead and Shorrock 1997: 11). Earlier, Zeichner and Tabachnick (1981) used the term 'wash out effect' to describe the force of these socializing influences, although more recently Furlong et al. (2000) have argued that initial training does exert a continuing influence on 'the forms of professionalism [new teachers] have the opportunity to develop and the knowledge, skills and values they acquire' (p. 29). These apparent contradictions are interesting, but what our research with the new teachers demonstrated was that what an individual brings to each new situation is of more importance. We also found that what they bring will vary enormously depending on their prior attitudes and experiences (see also Elbaz 1983;

Clandinin 1986). Thus, what new teachers bring to a particular school or class, together with the culture of that school, will help to shape their future professional development (Hargreaves and Fullan 1992), as will the strategies they adopt once in post in order to negotiate socialization processes.

Key findings and action points

This chapter has moved from using the model to understand the professional development of Fatou and Gina, to using it to develop understandings of your own development through:

- first, locating yourself in the model;
- then, reflecting on your professional development; and
- last, looking at ways of using research to develop your practice.

Teaching is an exciting career and understanding your own development is helpful in being able to move beyond survival. The model is a potentially useful way in which you can explore this, and Activity 9.2 explained a way in which you can go about it. What is important to keep in mind, though, is that you need to make the process of locating yourself in the model work for you. Use it to help you think about your professional development and to help you to better understand yourself.

As you develop professionally, try some of the research-based techniques introduced in this chapter. They will help you think about and develop your working practices and help you to challenge some of the more routinized elements of your professional work. The further reading and useful website section at the end of the chapter provides some very readable and supportive references to help you in this process. All contain lots of ideas to help you understand your practice in the classroom and its effects on children's learning.

Concluding discussion

You will find that in the first years of teaching you will have a very steep learning curve. This is especially so in your very first year in your new post. What we began to identify through our work with the new teachers was the importance of being able to transfer professional knowledge gained in one context to another (different) context, for example, from their final teaching practice to their first appointment. This was not always easy, as it involved being able to identify what was situationally specific in their prior experience, what would be useful and relevant in their new context and what they needed to do in order to 're-situate' knowledge in that new context. It was this that Fatou found hard when she changed to a Reception class after spending her training and NQT years with a Year 2 class.

Many authors stress the importance of being able to re-situate prior experience in this way and as Eraut (2002b: 4) says: 'Such re-situation is a learning process that involves both an understanding of the new situation and transformation of previous knowledge'. We saw in the first part of this book how this learning process was particularly challenging for Abbey as she described how she encountered in her first post so much that seemed to be different from her teaching practice. She was fortunate to have very supportive staff to help her through this learning process. Cathryn, on the other hand, had experiences in her training placement (e.g. with children with particularly challenging behaviour) which she was able to 're-situate' very easily within her new context. Understanding yourself as a teacher and being able to 'move beyond survival' does involve you being able to adjust or adapt what you have learnt to your new teaching context. This in turn involves you developing an understanding of yourself and your practice.

What happens next in terms of your professional learning and development in your early career depends on a range of factors as we have seen in this chapter. These factors involve you as well as the context in which you are working. Being able to identify and reflect on areas of strengths and further development is very important, but more than this, if you can make use of some of the ways suggested in this chapter to reflect on and improve practice, it will be more than just you who will benefit: your improved practice will affect the children with whom you work, as well as contribute to school improvement.

Further reading and useful website links

Altrichter, H., Posch, P. and Somekh, B. (1993) *Teachers Investigate Their Work: An Introduction to the Methods of Action Research.* London: Routledge.

Fielding, M. and Bragg, S. (2003) *Students as Researchers: Making a Difference.* Cambridge: Pearson Publishing.

Flutter, J. and Ruddock, J. (2004) *Consulting Pupils. What's in it for Schools.* London: RoutledgeFalmer.

Lewis, A. and Lindsay, G. (eds) (2000) *Researching Children's Perspectives.* Buckingham: Open University Press.

Rudduck, J. and Flutter, J. (2004) *How to Improve Your School.* London: Continuum.

Stoll, L., Fink, D. and Earl, L. (2004) *It's About Learning (and it's About Time) What's in it for Schools.* London: RoutledgeFalmer.

10
Dropping out and staying in

This chapter considers issues of retention with reference to current research findings. In relation to the early years of teaching, some of the reasons underlying staying in and dropping out of teaching are explored. More generally, the chapter also considers the main 'pushes and pulls' into and out of the profession.

Introduction

As we have seen throughout this book, new primary teachers progress in different ways for different reasons and at different rates during their first few years in teaching. In the first two chapters of this part of the book we also saw that professional development involves two main aspects, namely: the acquisition of teaching skills and the ability to manage professional demands. Moving beyond 'survival' was important for all new teachers, but this needed to occur in relation to both these aspects of professional development. From our research with the new teachers we found that although the acquisition of teaching skills was an essential factor in teacher progress, the ability to manage professional demands was often a more important factor in terms of influencing whether or not the new teachers were planning to 'stay in' or 'drop out' of teaching.

However, questions of retention are not straightforward. We saw in Gina's case that she had invested a tremendous amount in order to train as a teacher: first working part-time for a number of years to obtain a degree and then living away from her family for the PGCE year. Despite this, towards the end of her first year in teaching she was beginning to lose motivation as she was finding it difficult to manage the demands of her first post as well as juggle family and other commitments. However, Gina did not drop out of teaching. As we saw earlier in the book, she changed from full- to part-time for her second year. Then, when this arrangement did not work out well either due to her heavy workload and to the school frequently wanting her to work as a supply teacher on her non-working days, Gina decided to work as a supply teacher only during her third year. While working as a supply teacher she looked for another part-time job which better suited her needs. She eventually found a solution to managing the demands of teaching which worked for her and which enabled her to continue teaching and now works in a school which allows her to work the part-time hours she feels comfortable with.

In this chapter we will look in more detail at some of the reasons behind 'staying in' and 'dropping out' of teaching.

Issues in retention

It is possible to look at retention figures over the past few years and jump to conclusions about why teachers may leave the profession without looking in depth at their reasons for leaving. The media has, on occasion, painted a negative picture of teaching as a career and emphasized the high drop-out rate. But, in reality, is this the case?

As part of our research, we sent questionnaires to all the primary teachers who had trained in one institution during the 1990s and also carried out follow-up interviews with 32 of these teachers (see Studies 1 and 3 in the Appendix for further details as well as Table 10.1). We were interested in

Table 10.1 Survey of primary teachers trained at one institution during the 1990s: recruitment into teaching and retention

Year qualified	1991	1992	1993	1994	1995	1996	1997	1998	1999
Number of years after qualifying	10	9	8	7	6	5	4	3	2
Total numbers attaining QTS	56	65	65	62	66	57	51	23	24
Known destinations (totals)	24	20	26	22	26	28	26	23	24
Known destinations (%)	42.9	30.8	40.0	35.5	39.4	49.1	51.0	100.0	100.0
Number still teaching	20	13	20	16	20	24	20	17	24
Number left teaching	2	5	5	5	5	2	4	4	0
Number did not enter teaching	2	2	1	1	1	2	2	2	0
Of total known destinations:									
% still teaching	83.3	65.0	76.9	72.7	76.9	85.7	76.9	73.9	100.0
% left teaching	8.3	25.0	19.2	22.7	19.2	7.1	15.4	17.4	0.0
% did not enter teaching	8.3	10.0	3.8	4.5	3.8	7.1	7.7	8.7	0.0

finding out what these teachers were doing now. How many would still be teaching? How many may never have taught? The questionnaire and interview data provided a valuable snapshot of what was happening over this period within one case study institution. Our findings were similar to those of studies being carried out in different parts of the UK (e.g. Howson 2001).

One of the things which surprised us when we analysed the responses to the questionnaires was the small number of people in each year who had left teaching (between two and five each year) or who had never taught (one or two each year). We had expected that, over this period of time, there would have been a higher drop out rate, but this was not the case (see Table 10.1). (However, it should also be noted that this could have been a sampling effect, i.e. those that dropped out might be expected to be less likely to have responded to our questionnaire.) We then looked at the reasons people gave for leaving teaching or never entering teaching.

We found that the 32 people (14.6 percent of respondents) who had *left teaching* over the decade had done so for a range of reasons, including:

- family reasons which were either positive (e.g. would like to return to teaching after some time out) or negative (e.g. workload difficult to sustain with children);
- wanting to move into other area of work unconnected with teaching (e.g. business administration);
- wanting to move into other work connected with education but not teaching-related (e.g. LEA administration, educational psychology, museum work);
- long hours, stress, etc.;
- the climate of teaching, government changes, degree of prescription in primary teaching;
- feeling unsupported by their school;
- illness or accident.

In many cases, we found that a combination of the above reasons had led to a decision to leave teaching and rarely was this straightforward. In addition, not all the reasons given for dropping out were negative. As we can see from the list above, some people (usually women) left for family reasons, but they often expressed an intention to return to teaching after a career break, while others moved into work related to teaching.

Similarly, the 13 people (5.9 percent of the respondents) who *did not enter teaching* gave a range of reasons, some of which were also positive choices, including:

- went into a different occupation related to education (e.g. educational publishing);

- went abroad (not to teach);
- returned to their previous occupation because they felt it compared more favourably with teaching (usually in relation to workload, stress, salary);
- didn't obtain a teaching post on qualifying.

What about those people who were *still in teaching?* Seventy-nine percent of those who responded to the questionnaire (174 people) were still in teaching in the UK or overseas. What was particularly striking from the questionnaires and interviews was that the rewards of class teaching, especially working with the children, were overwhelmingly the main reason for teachers remaining in the profession.

Further analysis of the data revealed four main patterns of teaching career, which could be characterized as follows:

- *Traditional/incremental pattern*: the teacher moves up the career ladder, generally moving from school to school for promotion, eventually to headship.
- *Continuous pattern*: the teacher generally remains below senior management level and in the same school. This is often through their own choice.
- *Fragmented pattern*: the teacher makes frequent moves between schools, involving part-time, full-time and supply work, and may also take some time out of work (often female).
- *Sideways pattern*: the teacher moves into education-related work, often in senior positions (e.g. advisory work, literacy/numeracy consultants).

Because of concerns about the numbers of teachers leaving the profession, a number of other studies have been carried out into teacher retention. In a particularly worrying study, Smithers and Robinson (2001) found that, of every 100 final year teacher training students, 40 did not enter the profession, while a further 18 left during the first three years of teaching. These figures seem particularly high and are much higher than our findings above for the case study institution. On a positive note, the findings do not appear to have been repeated since (Smithers and Robinson 2003, 2004).

A larger survey (of 70,011 respondents) carried out by MORI found that 35 percent did not expect to be teaching in five years' time (GTC 2002). However, of these, more than half (52 percent) planned to retire. Of the others, 10 percent wanted to find alternative jobs still in education, some planned to raise a family (4 percent) and only 17 percent wanted to change professions altogether. Some of the teachers in our research, when asked where they saw themselves in five years' time, also expressed similar sentiments (although none said they were planning to retire, which was not surprising as our research focused more on teachers early in their careers). Some teachers' comments showed a real ambivalence. They were concerned about the workload, as for example this teacher explained:

> I don't think I'll be teaching. I look around at the staff in this school, and some are really experienced, and I think: 'Am I prepared to spend the next 40 years doing this?' I get so tired, and if experienced staff are still having to work such long hours, is that what I want? I love teaching, I love being with the children, I get a buzz when I see the children really progressing, so I'm thinking of supply work as you haven't got the paperwork, but then you don't get to build a relationship with the children ... The thing is [my partner] supports me so much, but why should he have to? Like this weekend, we're going into school to get my class ready for next term. I don't want the rest of my life to be like that. I'm seriously thinking of leaving at the end of the summer. I'm seeing a careers advisor next week, I'm even thinking of going into PA work.

Teachers' excessive workloads have been highlighted in a number of studies (e.g. GTC 2002). In this teacher's case, as with so many to whom we spoke, what created the dilemma was that they 'loved teaching'. So what leads to teachers dropping out or staying in?

Why do teachers drop out?

Although the majority of the teachers to whom we spoke were positive about teaching, there were a minority who were not. For instance, two teachers who had decided to leave teaching explained their reasons for leaving as follows:

> I've had enough, I'm hoping to go into marketing or advertising. I don't enjoy it at all here, I feel really cut off from the rest of the school ... I just think there is far too much work involved and not enough support given, so I'm going.

> The paperwork and the time spent on it. I have no time for myself, my partner, friends. I spend time feeling guilty about not spending even more time preparing lessons to make them more interesting. I even feel guilty about being ill and not working then. I've been ill over the holidays and I feel guilty that I haven't spent the time getting ready for school.

As we saw in Chapters 8 and 9, moving beyond 'survival' in relation to both the acquisition of teaching skills and the ability to manage the demands of teaching were essential if teachers were to feel a sense of satisfaction about their job. It seems that in both these teachers' cases they were struggling, mainly in relation to their ability to manage the demands of teaching. When we looked at other people's research, we found that the main reasons teachers tended to give for leaving the profession were a heavy workload, pupil behaviour which they found difficult to manage, government initiatives, poor pay, stress, low status, poor career prospects and resources (e.g. Smithers and Robinson 2001 in relation to secondary teachers; GTC 2002). Leicestershire County Council (LCC) have called these kinds of reasons negative 'push' factors (LCC 2003). They highlighted how individual push factors can simply remain a background irritation, but the problem comes when several are combined together (LCC 2003), then the effect of any one factor can become the last straw (see Figure 10.1). Research by the Audit Commission (2002) revealed that it is largely 'push' factors that lead teachers to leave their jobs, rather than the 'pull' of other careers and the Institute for Policy Studies in Education (Dalgety et al. 2003) found that the majority of teachers who drop out of the profession move into less well paid work.

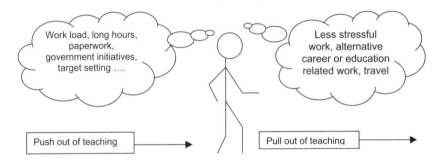

Figure 10.1 Pushes and pulls out of teaching

However, as we saw earlier in this chapter, it is important to remember that some moves out of teaching represent positive choices, for instance some teachers take a career break or travel abroad for a while. Others will take time out to raise children. In relation to those leaving secondary teaching in 2003, Smithers reported that 14.6 percent expressed the likelihood of returning to teaching at a later stage (HoC 2004b). In addition, some teachers move into further or higher education, independent schools or decide to go part-time or do supply teaching (White et al. 2003). Other research has indicated that while the proportion of qualified teachers who are teaching at any one point may be as low as 50 percent, 83 percent had taught at some point (Howson 2001). The House of Commons Select Committee which has undertaken a very thorough survey of teacher recruitment and retention in secondary schools has suggested that a balance of those with long-term careers in teaching, those who teach and move on to other work and those who enter teaching at a later stage is needed (HoC 2004a).

Why do teachers stay in teaching?

What is it that keeps teachers in teaching? What is it that stops them from dropping out? From our research, the three main answers to these questions were overwhelmingly, working with the children, the 'buzz' they got from teaching and, as the teacher above said, they just 'love teaching'. Developing the ability to manage professional demands was also important as we saw with Abbey, Cathryn, Fatou and Gina. The four teachers had their ups and downs in their first three years in teaching as they acquired skills and learnt to manage professional demands, but when we spoke to them at the beginning of their fourth year, they were all determined to stay in teaching. Why was this?

> I still want to go further and I do want to be a deputy, but some days I just think I am so comfortable here, why give it up, then other days I think, right, this is the day I'm going to go out and see what's there. I will do it, I will make deputy head. It was really just a personal choice, I decided early on that I wanted to do that. I've now been inspired by our current head.
>
> (Abbey)

> I'm science coordinator and I've just got into the gifted and talented bug that's going around, I'm also the DT coordinator, you see we're a small school so you've got to take on different roles. I was asked to be the science coordinator and I love that role but I've been doing that for a few years now so that's fairly easy. And with the DT coordinator I knew that the DT policy hadn't been updated for years and I said to the head 'I'm happy to have a go at it'. This is me now, I'm happy here, I think I'll be here for a long time.
>
> (Cathryn)

> I am the DT coordinator and have been since I started training, it's easy as I've done it since I started training, I also order the stationary for the school. Sometimes I think I may like to be part of the school's senior management team but then sometimes I look at what they do and think 'What's the point of all that work?' I'm filling in forms at the minute for threshold, but there's so much to fill in.
>
> (Fatou)

I intend to stay in teaching; the only time I ever think about leaving is in the summer when I think, 'Oh I'd rather be at home all day than being at work'. But that's not because I don't enjoy it, I'd think that no matter what I did! But I've got a friend in secondary and she is thinking of leaving, she did her NQT the same time as me but she has had far more difficulties, the [verbal] abuse she gets is awful, and she is finding it really hard.

(Gina)

As we can see from the four teachers' comments, they all get a 'buzz' from teaching. They are also all beginning to more realistically appraise what they do as well as thinking ahead in order to ensure they retain the 'buzz'. There are other factors too. Have a look at Activity 10.1 which focuses on factors that affect early career teachers.

Activity 10.1

Look again at Abbey's, Cathryn's, Fatou's and Gina's quotes above. At the end of three years in teaching they were all still enthusiastic and clearly intending to stay in teaching. What do you think were the main factors keeping them enthusiastic and wanting to stay in teaching?

Think about someone you trained with. Can you identify any times when they might have felt pushed or pulled out of teaching? What actions did they take and why?

Finally, think about your own situation and try to identify what factors have affected your feelings about teaching as a profession.

Working towards retention solutions

Concerns about teacher retention, among other issues, have led more recently to the government review and remodelling of the workforce. Ralph Tabberer of the TTA has stressed the need to make teaching a profession with more flexible working arrangements that will retain, for instance, more women with school-age children (HoC 2004b). The TTA has recently produced a guide focusing on effective practices in teacher retention, drawing on case studies and research findings (TTA 2003b) and the Teacher Support Network (2002) which is also looking at teacher retention, highlighted positive factors which would retain teachers.

Individual and collective solutions are both crucial. For example, Tim Brighouse has stressed the importance of teachers working together, learning from and supporting each other and Patrick Nash has emphasized the importance of organizational approaches, such as good management and leadership, which help to improve staff morale (Teacher Support Network 2002). These factors have also been identified by Ofsted (2002) and the TTA who additionally highlight the importance of investing time and money in retaining the expertise of staff and the need to create a positive environment where teachers feel valued. Perhaps most importantly though, it is the seemingly small factors that appear to make a real difference to staff morale on a day to day basis, and this is where the individual leadership styles of heads and senior managers can make a difference. For example, providing sandwich lunches for working meetings, family-friendly policies and 'no-bag' days when teachers are not allowed to take work home are all examples highlighted by the Teacher Support Network (2002).

The previous section in this chapter identified some of the pushes and pulls out of teaching, but it is important to also identify what may pull teachers back into teaching if they are thinking about dropping out, or have dropped out (see Figure 10.2). Leicestershire County Council (2003) identified the following factors that they felt might act as 'pulls' back into teaching:

- better workload management;
- improved work–life balance;
- empowerment and motivation;
- providing teachers with the tools to do the job.

It is highly likely that you can identify other 'pulls back' too.

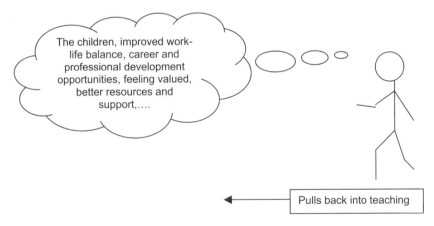

The children, improved work-life balance, career and professional development opportunities, feeling valued, better resources and support,....

Pulls back into teaching

Figure 10.2 Pulls back into teaching

Key findings and action points

In this chapter we have looked at:

- issues around teacher retention;
- why teachers drop out of teaching and why they stay in;
- ways in which we can work towards retaining more teachers.

What is important in all this is that understanding issues around retention is crucial not simply because we need to keep teachers in the profession who would otherwise have left, but as a genuine attempt to improve the working life of all teachers. This responsibility applies at all levels from individuals through to government policies. We need to ensure we are working in school communities which are person-centred.

Overwhelmingly the reasons given for staying in teaching were three-fold: working with the pupils, the 'buzz' of teaching and the sentiment often voiced to us by new teachers, 'I just love teaching'. Teaching was clearly perceived as an exciting profession that the new teachers were proud to be in. What was important in what they said was the need to get all the 'other things' right.

Action points

- Be clear about what you value in teaching as a profession. As for so many of the teachers to whom we spoke, it is important to become aware of what you value and then to be sure not to forget it.
- If you feel you are being either pulled or pushed out of teaching do something about it now. Talk to people, identify what factors you can do something about yourself and what you may need help with. Hold onto your values!

Concluding discussion

Teacher retention is not an easy issue but understanding what motivates teachers as well as understanding their concerns can be helpful. As we have seen, some of the reasons teachers gave for leaving the profession represented positive choices and some of those who left teaching intended to return. However, there are still too many teachers leaving the profession for negative reasons. We have seen that overwhelmingly the reason teachers gave for staying in teaching was the excitement of teaching itself.

At the end of their third year in teaching, Abbey, Cathryn, Fatou and

Gina were all still enthusiastic and enjoying teaching while also looking to new challenges. At the same time, however, they were appraising what this would mean in terms of their abilities to manage professional demands. As we have seen throughout this part of the book, the importance of 'moving beyond survival' in the early years of teaching is crucial. We found that it tended to be the minority of early career teachers who did not manage to do this, and they were the ones who were thinking about dropping out. Most new teachers, like Gina, managed to find solutions to difficulties they experienced in managing professional demands. The main 'pull' of the profession, which we found to be an exceptionally strong pull, remained the actual work with children and the excitement of teaching itself.

Further reading and useful website links

Fielding, M. (ed.) (2001) *Taking Education Really Seriously: Four Years' Hard Labour.* London: RoutledgeFalmer.
Fullan, M. and Hargreaves, A. (1992) *What's Worth Fighting for in Your School? Working Together for Improvement.* Buckingham: Open University Press.
Hargreaves, A. and Fullan, M. (1998) *What's Worth Fighting for in Education?* Buckingham: Open University Press.

The Becoming a Teacher Project funded by the Department for Education and Skills (DFES), General Teaching Council (GTC) and Teacher Training Agency (TTA) which may be found at: www.becoming-a-teacher.ac.uk

PART 4
Looking ahead

This final part of the book takes a look to the future by considering ways in which teachers' professional knowledge and skills may be enhanced and the different directions their careers may take. We do this by drawing on findings from all three of our research studies (see Appendix for details), especially the four case study teachers, Abbey, Cathryn, Fatou and Gina, whose progress we have followed throughout the book.

We look initially at where the beginning teachers see themselves in five years' time. As earlier in the book, we use the voices of the new teachers to help you to reflect on your own professional learning and development, this time looking ahead to possible shorter and longer term goals. Finally, we look ahead by considering the wider context of current and prospective changes in education, such as workforce remodelling and interschool networks, and the consequent implications for changes in the role of the primary teacher.

11
Professional development

This chapter looks to the future and considers what Abbey, Cathryn, Fatou, Gina and the other new teachers thought they would be doing in five years' time. Building on some of the ideas presented earlier in the book, this chapter reflects on professional goals and ways of working towards achieving them. The chapter also considers professional development and suggests activities which early career teachers may find helpful in supporting their own professional learning.

Introduction

What are your goals in teaching? Have you thought about how you see your professional life developing? Some new teachers have very clear ideas about what they are aiming to achieve in their teaching career. For instance, some enjoy classroom life itself and aim to broaden their experience within a phase of education and develop specific aspects of their teaching skills. They may, for example, want to become a subject coordinator. Other new teachers aim for management positions and want to become a deputy head or a head-teacher. Some new teachers are keen to undertake further training, perhaps to become an educational psychologist, or maybe a teacher of the deaf, while others aim to travel and teach abroad.

Teachers enter the profession with a range of interests, prior experiences, skills and knowledge acquired through life experiences as well as through their initial teacher training programme and their previous work experience. Their professional learning is shaped and developed, partly by what they bring to teaching, and partly through interactions with others in the workplace (colleagues, pupils, parents, etc.) and through the contexts within which they work. This is something that makes the profession interesting and enriches what we do.

Whether or not you have given thought to the professional goals you would like to achieve, you will without doubt have thought about your professional learning and development. As teachers, we are actively and continually involved in professional learning. We think about what we do and how our teaching impacts on pupil learning. Engaging in this kind of reflective practice makes us professional learners. In this chapter we will start by outlining where the new teachers to whom we spoke saw themselves in five years' time. We will then move on to consider your professional goals as well as focusing on ways of engaging with professional development and learning.

Looking to the future

We were interested to know about the future career aspirations of the teachers involved in our research and, as part of our questionnaires, we asked new teachers where they saw themselves in five years' time. When we analysed the questionnaire responses, we found that the majority of these beginning teachers (70 percent) saw themselves still teaching (see Table 11.1). Only a small proportion (6.2 percent) said they would not be teaching, with a further 3.1 percent giving family commitments as a reason for not teaching. Table 11.1 also shows that a significant minority (20.9 percent) of the new teachers were 'not sure' where they would be in five years' time.

Table 11.1   Where do newly qualified teachers see themselves in five years' time?

	Number	*Percentage*
Still teaching and having taken on extra responsibilities	52	40.3
Still teaching (with no extra responsibilities)	24	18.7
Part-time teaching	7	5.4
Teaching abroad	7	5.4
Not teaching	8	6.2
Not teaching because of children	4	3.1
Not sure	27	20.9
Total	**129**	**100**

We included a similar question in our interviews with new teachers. When asked to look to the future and tell us where they saw themselves in five years' time, we received expanded responses and explanations of some of their thinking:

> If I'm still in the same school as I'm in now, I can imagine myself either with year group responsibility or curriculum responsibility. My ambition is to stay as a classroom teacher rather than progress through the school, and then take on mentoring roles in the future.

> Long-term I want to be the music coordinator or early years coordinator but I'd also quite like to work my way [towards] nursery,

a nursery attached to a school, but I've got no ambition to work my way up to senior management or anything like that. I don't want to do anything that gives that sort of responsibility or that sort of extra work.

I'm happy to go on teaching just as I am. Maybe take on more bits of responsibility but I haven't got any desire to be head or deputy head or anything.

Whatever I do I'll move up the career ladder and I'll reach the top, or at least as high as I want to go. At the minute I'm thinking about VSO, or maybe just going somewhere to experience different cultures.

These quotes were typical of the responses we received when we talked to the new teachers. Although the majority still saw themselves in teaching, they were generally beginning to think more about whether they might want to take on additional responsibilities, and if so, what kind of responsibilities they would want. Some early career teachers were clear about wanting to remain in teaching as a class teacher, others were thinking more about a 'career ladder'. Only a few of the teachers said they saw themselves in, or working towards, senior management positions in five years' time.

Some teachers were thinking about teaching abroad for a while:

I think I would like to go abroad to teach. I'd work in a British school but I've planned to go to South-East Asia and America to teach there, I'm not quite sure when I'll go, but that's what I'm aiming to do.

Other new teachers were content to stay largely as they were:

I am very happy to stay in this school for a while. They're building a new school and I'd like to see that develop. A lot of people say I should move on and not stay in the same place but I'm really happy here so I don't see any reason for changing.

And some teachers, generally women, anticipated that in five years' time they would have changed from working full-time to working on a part-time basis.

Possibly working part-time. My children would prefer that … my husband is very busy as well, he works about 90 hours a week and I work 60 plus hours a week, so between us there's an awful lot of work, so I would love to think that I could work part-time.

> Well I think I'll probably still be a teacher with maybe a bit more responsibility, but in all honesty I'll probably be working part-time because I'll probably have started a family by then.

Lastly, there were a few new teachers, as we saw in Part 3 of this book, who were ambivalent about whether or not they would still be in teaching in five years' time, the ambivalence tending to be related to managing professional demands:

> Some days I think, 'Yes, I will stay in teaching' and other days I'm overwhelmed by the amount of work there is to do, there is a massive workload that comes with teaching.

So, many of the new teachers not only saw themselves in teaching in five years' time, but were also beginning to think about longer term professional goals. Managing professional demands still tended to be one of their main concerns and seemed to be an influencing factor for those contemplating additional responsibilities, for instance, it was often the main reason given by those who were not aspiring to senior management positions. In the next section, we will look at how Abbey, Cathryn, Fatou and Gina responded when asked where they saw themselves in five years' time.

A return to the casestudies

In the previous section of this chapter we considered how teachers responded towards the beginning of their second year in teaching when asked where they saw themselves in five years' time. We saw in Chapter 10 that after three years in teaching, Abbey, Cathryn, Fatou and Gina were still enthusiastic about and intending to stay in teaching. We then asked them what they thought they would be doing in five years' time. Timing can make a difference to a new teacher's response to this question. In relation to these four teachers, they were confident about their developing teaching skills and how to manage professional demands.

In Abbey's case, we saw in Chapter 10 that after being in teaching for three years, not only did she want to remain in teaching, but she was one of the few teachers who had also expressed an interest in senior management posts. Abbey was being inspired by her headteacher in this. When asked at the beginning of her fourth year specifically where she saw herself in five years' time, Abbey responded initially by saying that she wanted to become a deputy headteacher, however, having reflected on this she considered that this may be rather ambitious and stated:

> Maybe as literacy coordinator or something like that, I'm not into big style fast-tracking. I know I could earn a lot more money if I did, but … I'm not sure whether [becoming a deputy head] will be as quick as five years because there is so much to learn, but I will certainly be on my way up.

It seemed that the more Abbey was learning, the more she realized there was to learn. She had always been ambitious, even in her first year of teaching she had ambitions about being promoted to deputy head. However, after she had been teaching for three years, although her long-term ambition was still to become a deputy head, she realized that she would need to work towards this. She decided that one of the steps she could take would be to take responsibility for a major area of the curriculum and aimed to become a literacy coordinator as a short-term goal.

When Cathryn was asked where she would be in five years' time, however, she revealed that she was still strongly focused on classroom teaching itself:

> Still in the classroom. I've got no aspirations to be a head or a deputy head. If this job continues as it is I would be happy to be here for the next ten years.

In Cathryn's case, she was happy as a class teacher and not looking for additional senior management responsibilities.

Fatou however had been a design and technology coordinator and had thought about taking on a senior management role in the future, but when asked specifically to think about five years hence, she talked about the dilemma of the 'higher up you go, the less time you spend in the classroom':

> I don't really know, I like being a classroom teacher but the thing is, the more you take on and the higher up you go, the less time you spend in the classroom. I wouldn't mind being something like an art coordinator but I do like to know what's going on in the school, so I could see myself helping with lots of different things, helping different teachers with different clubs so I could get involved in lots of little things. I'd rather do that than put my energies into one area.

Last there was Gina who had changed from working full-time to a part-time post in order to reduce the professional demands placed on her and to enable her to manage both her professional and personal life more easily. However, she anticipated that she would have increased her teaching hours in five years' time, although she was not sure apart from this, what she would be doing:

I may be teaching more by then because my children will be older ... I've got mixed feelings at the minute, I'm not sure where I'll be in five years' time.

Thus, all four of these new teachers at the start of their fourth year in teaching were thinking confidently about the future and about future professional goals. Their personal situations and the professional contexts in which they work have helped to shape their views; their awareness of this underpins any uncertainty about what they would like to be doing and what they thought they would be doing in five years' time.

In addition to personal and professional contexts, the landscape of teaching itself changes and this brings new opportunities as well as new challenges. For instance, the late 1980s and the 1990s brought the National Curriculum to England and Wales, followed by the National Literacy Strategy (NLS) and the National Numeracy Strategy (NNS). More recently (2003) the Primary National Strategy, which takes the NLS and NNS under its umbrella, has brought additional developments to primary teaching. Chapter 12 will return to the changing landscape of teaching in more detail, but it is important here to keep in mind that education does not stand still. As one newly qualified teacher said to us towards the end of their first year:

Well what I've noticed is that things keep changing and my school are keen on [subject] integration and we may go back to integrated days in the future and I won't know how to do it. Education will keep changing, I've noticed it swings one way and then swings back again and there'll be a time probably when literacy and numeracy hours go, well probably not altogether but they won't be like they are now, less structured perhaps. Particularly with our [training] year, our cohort, with the focus on literacy and numeracy, people say things about topic maths and we don't know what that means.

Things do change in education as this new teacher identified, but you are not on your own in this. Working with colleagues in schools can help you develop professionally and help you adapt to any changes as and when they occur.

Thinking about the future: professional goals

What will *you* be doing in five years' time? Do you think you will be teaching in the same or in a different school? Will you be working full- or part-time? Perhaps you will have taken on additional responsibilities? If so, what would you like these responsibilities to be? Have a go at Activity 11.1 which aims to enable you to reflect on what you would like to be doing in five years from now as well as to help you consider some of the factors which may influence you.

Activity 11.1

Start by thinking about where you see yourself in five years' time. If you are not too sure, then think about the options available to you and the various things you may like to be doing then.

What influenced your thoughts? Some of these influences may be personal (e.g. family or other personal commitments), some may be professional (e.g. having engaged successfully with an aspect of pupil learning or maybe recent teaching experiences in school), some influences may result from working with an inspirational colleague (e.g. on an area of the curriculum) and some may be because of a particular interest of yours (e.g. an aspect of special educational needs or perhaps a certain subject area).

Once you have decided on where you would like to be in five years' time, or at least have an idea of the options that appeal to you, think about what steps you need to take to help you move towards your goal? What experiences do you need to gain? How will you do this? You may find it helpful to talk to a more experienced colleague who is working in an area that is of interest to you, and ask them about how their career has developed and what influenced them along the way.

Remember, working towards a long-term goal can be a lengthy process. When planning how to achieve your goal it may be necessary to break the pathway towards it down into small, manageable steps.

It is likely that when you have completed Activity 11.1 and thought carefully about the factors which influenced your thoughts you will have been able to identify that some of these factors will be enhancing factors, in other words, they will enhance your chances and support you in achieving your goal. Other factors will be restraining factors: they will restrain you from achieving your goal. Examples of enhancing factors are supportive or inspirational colleagues, good subject knowledge in the area you wish to develop or effective (professional) learning experiences. Examples of restraining factors are lack of opportunity or of appropriate learning experiences, unsupportive or maybe unhelpful colleagues, or lack of time.

In addition to these factors there is also sometimes an element of luck involved. For instance, at times you will hear colleagues explain a new development or promotion in terms of 'I was lucky, just in the right place at the right time'. However, it is likely to be more than 'luck' as without careful preparation that person may not have been in a position to take advantage of the opportunity which came along.

So how do you prepare yourself? Thinking ahead as we have done through Activity 11.1 is one way and we can illustrate this partly through Abbey's experiences. As we have seen earlier in the book, Abbey aspired to deputy headship. Although sometimes this goal was stronger than at other times, her general direction has always been towards a management position. She had three strong enhancing factors: supportive colleagues, an inspirational head and her own interest and drive to achieve this goal. However, the more experienced she became as a teacher and the more she learnt, the more she realized she had to learn. Because of all these factors, she realized that to take on a middle management position would be a useful and sensible step towards her goal. And even then she was cautious as we saw above adding, 'I'm not sure whether [becoming a deputy head] will be as quick as five years because there is so much to learn, but I will certainly be on my way up'. Abbey also took time to find out what knowledge, skills and abilities would be required of her and what other attributes would be desirable in an application for deputy headship. She is now ensuring she extends her experiences with this in mind. Abbey may well apply for deputy headship, perhaps in a smaller school, within the next few years, but when she does, she will be well prepared due to the time and thought she has put into planning her career development.

So far in this chapter we have focused mainly on career goals, although it is important to think ahead in these terms so that you are prepared for the opportunities which present themselves, it is also very important to think about your current practice, about your more immediate professional goals and what professional development will help your current working practices.

Professional development is much more than career aspiration. How you develop yourself professionally involves a focus on, for example, your teaching skills, your professional knowledge, your understanding of teaching and learning, your understanding of the social contexts of classrooms, on how pupils interact in the classroom and the playground, on how teachers and pupils interact and how all this affects learning. The list is endless; teaching is a profession where you never stop learning. How will you tackle this? How do you develop professionally? Before reading on have a go at Activity 11.2. Rather than looking longer term at possible career paths and aspirations, this activity aims to help you to identify your current professional development needs. The two (i.e. career aspirations and current professional development needs) are interrelated, but for this next task we will be focusing on the more immediate, on a shorter term, professional development focus.

Activity 11.2

Think about the school in which you are currently working and your current class or group of pupils. Take a moment or two to think about yourself in different situations with the pupils, think about the pupils themselves and how they behave in different contexts. For example, think about their behaviour and how you manage this during each of the following: practical sessions; whole class teaching sessions; group work activities; structured sessions; unstructured sessions; break and lunch times; assemblies; at the beginning and at the end of the day.

- Where do your strengths lie?

- Are there any areas you would like to develop further?

   Now think about the learning activities that take place during each of these sessions. Are you confident that all pupils achieve their potential in each of these situations? Again, consider:

- Where do your strengths lie?

- Are there any areas you would like to develop further?

   Remember, if there are areas of your work that you would like to address and improve upon, do not expect to become an 'expert' overnight. Work towards improving your practice in manageable steps, as we discussed in Chapter 9 – *think small!*

Once you have identified your professional development focus, you need to decide how you are going to work on it.

Engaging with professional development and learning

In Chapter 9 we introduced ways in which you could use reflection and some of the methods of action research to improve your practice in the classroom. We looked at two examples of research that early career teachers had carried out into their own classroom practices. Their aim was to improve teaching and learning. In this section of the chapter we will explore some of the ways in which professional development activities can make a difference to the pupils with whom you work as well as help you tackle your own professional goals.

   The sorts of activities suggested in Chapter 9 can be used by teachers working on their own to develop their practice. However, working with others can make the activities more productive. Both the teachers in Chapter 9 worked with another person, not in the classroom itself, but to talk through and suggest ways of going about the research, to plan how to carry it out and then to discuss the data and what the teachers appeared to be finding out about their own teaching and their pupils' learning.

It is highly likely that you have already discovered in your working life that collaboration can improve both the product and also the process of working. Planning together, sharing ways of working, observing each other, exchanging ideas for teaching and problem-solving with colleagues are just a few of the ways in which teachers work together. Working collaboratively can be with colleagues from within the school as well as with external specialists such as advanced skills teachers (ASTs).

Recent research by Cordingley et al. (2003) has highlighted how some kinds of continuing professional development (CPD) activities can be of particular benefit to teachers, notably those where teachers are learning from each other, where the focus is geared directly to day to day practices and where the activities profit both teachers and pupils. In most of the more effective forms of professional development activities teachers tended to work with external experts (e.g. ASTs or individuals from universities or the LEA) on activities linked directly to school-based work. In addition the emphasis in some of the more effective CPD activities was on peer support (rather than being led by an external expert), and where teachers were enabled to identify their own professional focus as well as to embed new practices over time. The point here is that it is not always necessary to do what some of the new teachers said they would need to do, i.e. 'go on a course', professional development can happen within your own school through working collaboratively with others. Some schools, for example, now encourage their staff to conduct small-scale research projects and make use of expertise, often in the form of a university-based colleague who spends time in a school working with teachers on school-based projects.

So, if the CPD was identified as effective, what impact did it have on the teachers? Cordingley et al. (2003) found four main reported changes in teachers' behaviour: teachers were more confident, they had an increased belief in their own effectiveness (in relation to pupil learning), they were more enthusiastic about collaborative working (despite having felt concerned initially about being observed) and they were found to be more committed to changing their practice and more willing to try new ways of working. This is important and we saw in Chapter 9 that the two teachers who engaged in their research were enthused and keen to try new things as a result of the activities they had undertaken to help them reflect more on their work.

As noted above, not all professional development need involve collaborative work with people external to your school. The National College for School Leadership (NCSL), for instance, emphasizes the importance of peer coaching, an approach which is based on trust between the teachers involved and aims to eliminate, as far as possible, the power dimensions that may exist between an external 'expert' and the teacher in the school. To be effective, however, the dialogue needs to be reflective and you need to ask questions of your practice and of its impact on learning. In order to support what they call an analytical conversation, the NCSL suggest a pre-lesson discussion and collaborative planning as well as video recording and observing of the lesson taught by one of the peer coaching partnership. The observation notes and the video recording are then used to support the post-lesson discussion (Leat undated). The approach is much like that of Example 1 in Chapter 9, but with the involvement of more than one teacher. This is certainly an approach which you will find useful but it is important to remember that you and your teacher-partner need to start by identifying the focus of the peer coaching exercise, keeping in mind that to be effective the focus should be both small and manageable. You can make use of Activity 11.2 to help you in this.

As they engage in this kind of professional development, teachers often look for professional recognition for the work that they do. Apart from re-cognition within the teacher's own school, currently more formal recognition of professional development activities has generally been through academic accreditation and further qualifications, often post-graduate certificates, di-plomas or Masters degrees. More recently the General Teaching Council (GTC) has developed the Teacher Learning Academy and a framework which aims to provide more coherent professional and academic recognition. Their website describes their work as follows:

> The GTC Teacher Learning Academy provides professional recogni-tion for teachers' professional learning, with the option of academic accreditation, with a particular focus on learning embedded within daily practice ... It aims to stimulate learning experiences for tea-chers which are effective for them, their pupils, their schools and for the education service. It seeks to support learning communities within and beyond schools that enrich teaching practice and support innovation.
>
> (GTC 2005)

A number of LEAs and universities have, and are, developing partnerships to take the initiatives forward. At the time of writing there is much happening on the horizon so this is something to keep an eye on (e.g. look at informa-tion from your LEA, local college or university and the GTC).

Key findings and action points

In this chapter we have looked to the future to consider:

- professional goals;
- professional development and learning;
- ways of identifying and tackling your professional development needs.

It is useful to think ahead early and begin to consider what direction you might like your career to take. Thinking about what you may like to do in the future enables you to begin to plan how you can achieve this, although along the way you may change direction. It is also helpful to start to think about what opportunities exist. For example, becoming an AST is the kind of professional goal now increasingly attractive to teachers who wish to teach rather than become senior managers.

But what about the development of your knowledge, skills and abilities? As we saw in this chapter, you will find that engaging in collaborative professional development activities, focused on school-based and day to day practices can be extremely productive. For primary teachers early in their careers, a key factor in the effectiveness of the activities tends to be the trust developed between those who collaborate. So, while you are still building confidence as a beginning teacher, it is important to keep this in mind.

Action points

- Think ahead and try to identify your goals in teaching and what is important to you.
- Think about where you will need to focus your energies when engaging in professional development activities.
- Plan to work collaboratively with colleagues rather than on your own.
- Make sure you establish the focus for your professional development. You cannot work on everything at once.

Concluding discussion

We all come into teaching with a range of skills and experiences and we all have different strengths and areas we wish to develop. In addition, the act of teaching and just being in the classroom raises many more questions: what do I need to do to ensure all of the pupils are engaged with this new topic? Why did the pupils react as they did to that last task? When is the best time to introduce this new way of working, and how should I go about it? How can I ensure the pupils understand what they need to do? How will I know that they do understand? And so on. Professional development and learning activities help us engage with our questions, generate new and more interesting questions and also tackle our target areas.

The kinds of activities you may find helpful in supporting your professional learning will vary. Some possibilities were discussed in this chapter. In addition, many teachers like to accredit their professional development activities, but what is of most importance is to keep in mind the purpose of what you are doing, to remember to keep your own professional development and learning in focus. Remember that the purpose of engaging in professional development is to improve your understanding, knowledge and skills, to develop your practice and its impact on pupil learning. Think small, be focused, work with colleagues and enjoy it!

Further reading and useful website links

Hart, S., Dixon, A., Drummond, M.J. and McIntyre, D. (2004) *Learning Without Limits*. Maidenhead: Open University Press.
MacGilchrist, B. and Buttress, M. (2004) *Transforming Learning and Teaching*. London: Paul Chapman.
Muijs, D. and Reynolds, D. (2005) *Effective Teaching*, 2nd edn. London: Sage.

Also see

National College for School Leadership http://www.ncsl.org.uk/
The DFES Standards website http://www.standards.dfes.gov.uk/primary/
The General Teaching Council's Teacher Learning Academy website
    http://www.gtce.org.uk/cpd_home/TLA/

12
Changing landscapes in primary education

This chapter looks ahead and considers possible developments and transformative practices in primary education in the light of current initiatives and educational thinking. School remodelling, school networks and the children's agenda are discussed and the implications of these changes for primary teaching are explored.

Introduction

Teaching is on the brink of some major changes over the next few years with workforce remodelling and other initiatives following hard on the heels of the national strategies and other centralized measures which dominated education during the late 1990s and early years of the twenty-first century. There are also a number of collaborative and multi-professional developments which could lead to major transformations in how professionals work in and across a range of educational contexts.

This final chapter of the book looks at some of these imminent changes in the light of their possible impact on the primary teacher's role. At this stage there are many questions we could ask. For example, how will the Children's Agenda affect the ways in which we work with other professionals in schools? How will the changing role of teaching assistants affect the work of teachers in primary school? How will all these changes impact on the children?

Although we cannot know how many of the teachers whose experiences we have drawn on in the book will remain in teaching or what those who remain will do, we can make some predictions about how their lives as teachers may be changed in the coming decade.

Looking backwards and forwards

The last ten years have seen immense changes in primary education in England and Wales. In the 1990s, cross-curricular topic work was the norm and there were concerns about falling standards culminating in a government enquiry on primary education and the 'Three Wise Men' report (Alexander et al. 1992), which criticized the then current teaching methods.

In previous chapters we have touched on the impact of the national literacy and numeracy strategies (DfEE 1998, 1999), which introduced a structured approach to the teaching of English and mathematics in primary schools, with a designated hour for each. This initiative was not always easy for experienced teachers to adapt to as they had to change the more fluid approach to the curriculum that they had used before, and many teachers felt de-skilled in the process. There were also concerns that non-core subjects were being squeezed out of the curriculum and that the literacy hour in particular left no room for more creative approaches to the teaching of English. In spite of these criticisms, however, standards in both English and mathematics at key stage 2 rose steadily for five years, although more recently they have remained fairly static.

Alongside the new strategies, a new culture of accountability was introduced, including standard assessment tasks (SATs) at key stages 1 and 2, target setting and school league tables, all with the aim of pushing standards up. Ofsted inspections 'named and shamed' failing schools and the number of teachers leaving the profession rose dramatically (Smithers and Robinson 2001; Audit Commission/Ofsted 2002). Increased centralization, heavy workloads and pressure arising from the initiatives and paperwork were cited among the reasons for teachers wanting to leave.

As a counterbalance to some of the criticisms of the strategies, the government document, *Excellence and Enjoyment* (DfES 2003b), heralded the introduction of the national primary strategy, which gave more autonomy to primary schools in delivering the curriculum, building on their strengths and developing innovative practice. This has led to the creative arts and cross-curricular work beginning to be reinstated, but with the structure and importance of literacy and numeracy still firmly in place. It is a mark of the resilience and flexibility of primary teachers that they have not only taken on board these recent changes, but transformed them in positive ways. You will have seen examples of this kind of transformation in your own schools in the particular ways in which teachers have interpreted and implemented the strategies or moved beyond them.

In spite of the many changes that education in the UK has gone through over the last decade, education policies and practices continue to develop. The teaching profession as a whole is currently undergoing major changes, including workforce remodelling and interprofessional practices to meet the children's agenda. The Teacher Training Agency has widened its remit to encompass continuing professional development of teachers as well as initial training, and Ofsted inspections are moving to a more self-evaluative approach. There are also many other broader educational developments which herald new, more collaborative ways in which schools and professionals in education can work together to share and extend good practice.

If we look ahead, these developments will all have a huge impact on schools and teachers in ways that we cannot yet foresee. Let's have a look at some of these changes in more detail in order to identify their possible impact and the implications for primary teachers in the next decade, as well as possibly further into the future.

School and workforce remodelling

The government aim of raising standards, together with the realization that teacher workloads were reaching unmanageable proportions, were put together in a national agreement (2003) to deliver joint action on these two areas. Changes to teachers' contracts were phased in from 2003–05, including limits to the time teachers can cover for absent colleagues, removal of some administrative and other tasks such as putting up displays, and guaranteed non-contact time for planning and preparation during the school day. Teaching assistants are taking on greater roles within the school as part of teams of adults delivering the curriculum, led by teachers themselves. Whole-school approaches are needed to plan and implement these dramatic changes and, in some areas, local steering groups have been formed to help support schools, with groups of schools and local education authorities taking a lead in coordinating and sharing good practice.

One of the key aims of workforce remodelling is to free up teachers to plan and teach more fully, rather than feeling that they are bogged down with administrative tasks. As we saw in Chapter 5, many new teachers feel that they are overwhelmed with the amount of paperwork required at the moment, so any moves to reduce this will be welcome. Non-contact time has been limited in many primary schools, so the introduction of guaranteed planning, preparation and assessment (PPA) time is a novelty in the UK, even though teachers in Europe have enjoyed it for years. An associated aim of remodelling is to recognize the expertise of all staff within a school and to use that expertise where it should be focused: on the children's learning and well being. There is also an increasing realization that teachers need to have a good work–life balance in order to be able to carry out their role fully and positively, and it is hoped that remodelling will help bring this about.

In some schools teachers are already benefiting from the protection of planning and preparation time. However, this and the move to more collaborative team approaches is likely to necessitate a shift in the culture of some schools, with consequent implications for new teachers. For example, although primary schools have recognized the importance of teaching assistants for many years, we saw in Chapter 7 how their role has already moved to a fuller partnership and higher status. Ever since the introduction of the literacy strategy, learning support assistants have been of increasing importance in working with individual children or groups, for example on phonics or other language work. Stronger moves towards inclusive approaches in schools have also resulted in teaching assistants playing an increased role in working with individuals and groups of pupils with additional learning needs. All teachers are now expected to plan for and work alongside teaching assistants.

However, we also saw in Chapter 7 how difficult many beginning teachers in our studies found it to take on what they saw as essentially a managerial role in their working relationships with teaching assistants (TAs). Sometimes it was those who had been teaching assistants themselves who found it easier to understand how TAs can be employed effectively in the classroom, and also found it easier to build positive working relationships with them. New teachers, particularly those coming into teaching straight from college, may need support and further training if they are to manage this aspect of their professional role effectively. Training is already under way in many parts of the country to enable TAs to take on higher level tasks and this is an essential part of the partnership.

All these changes carry financial implications which have to be addressed if the remodelling and related initiatives are to be a success. The signs so far are positive ones: the sense of freeing teachers up from aspects of their job which are burdensome has given many schools and their staff renewed enthusiasm, as has the sense that each school can take on the changes in a way that works for them. Although primary schools have always retained their individuality, we may find that there is an increased diversity of approach towards the implementation of remodelling, which could enrich the culture of primary schools and by implication, also enrich the primary teacher's role.

Before we move on to another recent development, take a look at Activity 12.1 which focuses on the remodelling agenda and how it may be affecting you and your school.

Activity 12.1

First, think about the impact that remodelling is having within your school and what difference it has already made to your own and other teachers' working lives, as well as to the roles of support staff. For instance, what impact is the introduction of designated non-contact PPA time having on teachers? Has this freed you up to do more planning and marking within working hours? Are you getting more help with administrative tasks?

Have any new challenges arisen as a result of these changes? For instance, are there different expectations in relation to the amount and type of work you are required to do? Is there a change in the number and type of meetings that

Activity 12.1 *cont.*

are now being held? How is this altering your relationships with other teachers, teaching assistants, parents or other professionals? Above all, is it
making any difference to the way that you work with the children in your
class?

School networks and learning communities

We have focused a great deal throughout the book on different ways that new
teachers can learn from more experienced colleagues. Beginning teachers can
develop professionally from working cooperatively or collaboratively in
school with other teachers, for instance on joint activities or on action research projects. As well as in-school collaboration, there are many developments in interschool collaboration. For example, we mentioned earlier that
some schools are grouping together, often under the coordination of local
education authorities, to share developments and practice in terms of school
remodelling. This kind of collaboration is also being forged more widely,
following the introduction of the primary (and, at secondary level, key stage
3) strategy, with the development of school networks and learning
communities.

Networks are not exclusive to schools, but are used widely in other organizations. In the school context, networks have been found to be useful in
sharing good practice, broadening the expertise of teachers and consequently
improving teaching and learning (DfES 2004b). They can provide a way of
finding out what is happening in different schools and improving learning
opportunities for pupils:

> School-to-school networks which are focused on learning offer a
> foundation for genuine transformation based on the knowledge
> embedded in teaching practice.
>
> (DfES 2004b: 2)

So what exactly are school networks and network communities and how
do they work? Networked learning communities are often across a range of
schools within an LEA or region; for instance, one network consists of a
secondary school and its feeder primary schools, focusing on assessment for
learning (AfL). Putting assessment for learning into practice became the pupil
and adult learning focus of the network. Teachers across the network were
trained in assessment for learning approaches and staff from the schools
worked together putting ideas into practice in their classroom. Another network learning community is focusing on accelerated learning and multiple

intelligence theories. Networks are also built between mainstream and special schools, their development being linked to their purpose and focus. At the time of writing the government is promoting networks as part of the Primary Strategy (DfES 2004b) with local education authority involvement.

How do we know if school networks are successful and what makes them work well? The NCSL suggests that effective networks can enable schools and teachers to share ideas and resources, develop wider relationships, solve problems together and develop innovative practices (www.ncsl.org.uk/ networked_learning). To be successful school networks need a clear purpose and rationale based on children's needs, and the adults involved should have a genuine interest in the focus of the network. Networks should ideally involve all members of the community including staff, parents and pupils. They are characterized by school to school visits and meetings, and other opportunities for teachers from the schools involved to meet, informally as well as formally, in order to build trust and encourage cooperation. Collaborative activities can include:

- joint working groups or project teams;
- focus groups;
- joint staff inset days;
- structured school to school visits;
- coaching and mentoring within and across schools.

As well as these kinds of activities, strong leadership and facilitation have been found to be particularly important in enabling networks to work effectively.

In addition to evaluations of individual networks, a DfES project looking at how good practice is transferred from teachers and schools to other practitioners (Fielding et al. 2005) has explored the nature of partnerships between schools and teachers, for instance: between advanced skills teachers and the partners with whom they work. The project looked at the challenges of these relationships and the way that practices were actually transferred or 'jointly developed' as teachers worked together and learnt from each other. It found that trusting relationships are at the heart of any collaborative or transfer process, and that time is needed to develop these. The support of school leadership is also vital if the joint development of practice is to take place between schools.

The implications for beginning and experienced teachers of this kind of collaborative working are clearly enormous. Not only are you going to be part of your own school planning and evaluation processes, but you may well be involved in a larger network of schools, all tackling a particular issue or problem and seeking joint answers, which will hopefully improve your own practice and the children's learning. This is potentially very exciting because, as with school remodelling, it potentially puts more power and independence into the hands of teachers themselves to change and improve practice. It also provides opportunities to widen teachers' knowledge and expertise through working with teachers from different school contexts.

However, as with any new way of working, there are also potential challenges or even perceived threats. How will you work together across schools? You may find, as a new teacher, that these kinds of new initiatives are a little overwhelming at first, especially while you are focused on the immediate demands of your own class early in your career. You will already be busy building relationships with other teachers, support staff and parents in your own school. Much will depend on your previous experiences. You may find that other teachers in your school share your enthusiams or anxieties. As well as the potential benefits of working with teachers in your own school, working together on a project that goes beyond your school to a wider context may actually help you to develop professionally in ways that you may not foresee in advance, and may enable you to come back to your own situation with a fresh eye. As with going on external courses, collaborative working through a network can be a way of renewing enthusiasm and giving you new ideas.

Integrated service provision and interprofessional work

One example of the way in which a collaborative and more integrated approach is beginning to work is through the development of extended schools. For a number of years community schools and colleges have been operating across the country. Provision varies but may include parents coming in to take programmes of study, children attending a breakfast or after-school club, or community groups using school buildings for their meetings. The success of these enterprises among others has led to the development and gradual extension of this widening range of services to eventually include all schools in England, with local education authorities playing a key role.

A pilot programme has already been running in six local education authorities, and will extend to all LEAs from the end of 2005. Schools will be asked to work with pupils and parents to identify a range of local needs that the school could help to deliver. For instance in one LEA schools are developing after-school care where this has not previously been offered; another school is developing a nature reserve in the school grounds, in collaboration with a local conservation group, which will be open to the whole community. The aim is to make the best use of school buildings, playgrounds and playing fields for as long as possible each day, rather than just using them for the limited time that pupils attend lessons.

Another example of more integrated, community-based services is the greater provision of neighbourhood nurseries, providing full day care and pre-school education for children aged three months to five years. Some nurseries have already further developed into day centres, offering parents and their children a range of services, including healthcare, benefits advice and access courses. These day care services are sometimes integrated within extended primary schools; in these cases, the range of services offered to families may be further widened to include such aspects as speech and language support or parenting classes. In other areas, community centres may be the preferred location. Whatever the setting, day care provision of this kind is seen as an important part of the local community, serving the needs of the local residents.

In order to offer as full a range of services as possible through the kind of provision outlined above, a number of professionals will be needed to deliver this variety of advice, training and education. Social workers, health visitors, nursery nurses and teachers are just some of the many people who will be needed to staff day care centres or extended schools and work collaboratively on particular projects or day to day matters. Voluntary organizations are also at the heart of this kind of initiative and project coordinators may be drawn from these as well as from paid professionals.

Collaboration and interprofessional working are at the heart of a related set of initiatives, derived from the government green paper, *Every Child Matters* (DfES 2003a), which suggests new ways in which we should work together to meet the needs and welfare of children and young people. A key aspect of this approach sets out plans for a range of integrated services, including education, health and social work. The government's aim is for every child, whatever their background or their circumstances, to have the support they need to be healthy, stay safe, enjoy and achieve through learning, make a positive contribution to society and achieve economic well being (DfES 2004a). This development constitutes a fundamental shift in the ways in which some schools and professionals have been working, but builds on already developing integrated service provision. Some areas of the country have begun to develop integrated services, some co-located within the community. You may well be working in such an area. Have a look at Activity 12.2 which aims to help you to think about your role and how it may develop as a result of changes to working practices.

Activity 12.2

First, think about whether your school is involved in any way in integrated service provision. If so, how and in what ways? Are there particular projects with which the school is involved, either as part of a network of schools or with other professionals or voluntary organizations in the community?

Activity 12.2 *cont.*

Now think about yourself and your role, or possible role, in this. What kind of knowledge or skills do you think you may need? Do you have the knowledge and skills needed to take part yourself? What further training or professional development might you need to help you to take part fully in this kind of initiative? What will this mean in terms of your role as a primary teacher?

All this may be further into your future development as a teacher, or you may already be working in a school which is fully or partially involved with integrated service provision or networks like the ones we have described. It is important to begin to consider how you might work with other schools, or alongside other professionals and project workers, to support the needs and interests of children and their families in a wider way. These kinds of collaborative practices are likely to transform the ways in which teachers work in the future and it is important to think now and be prepared for these developments yourself.

Key findings and action points

This chapter has looked at some important initiatives and other developments which will have implications for the ways in which teachers work in the future. The initiatives included:

- school and workforce remodelling;
- school networks and learning communities;
- integrated service provision.

We have seen some examples of how these more innovative practices may impact on schools and teachers and also how, as an individual teacher, you need to prepare for these changes. For example, school remodelling should give you more time within the school day to work on planning and assessment, and thus enable you to more easily collaborate with colleagues. You will need to learn how to plan for and work alongside other adults in the school such as teaching assistants and understand how they can enhance your joint contribution to the children's learning.

If your school is part of a network or learning community, you will have opportunities to take part in some innovative projects and you will also be able to work with teachers in other schools to solve problems or develop resources in particular areas of the curriculum. This will help you to extend your own knowledge and understanding and to develop areas in which you may currently feel under-confident. However, you will need to be well organized and learn to prioritize your work in order to fit this into an already busy schedule.

Similar issues arise with other developments, such as the delivery of integrated services to meet the children's agenda. Involvement in these developments will broaden your understanding and experience of how other professionals such as healthcare workers or social workers work with children, and how their role can contribute to children's development and well being.

Action points

- Plan how to make best use of PPA time, for example: working with teachers and other adults in the school to plan and assess children's learning.
- Find out about any collaborative projects that the school is involved in, for instance through school networks, and how you can contribute.
- Use the opportunities within your school to broaden your knowledge and experience as far as possible, particularly working with colleagues and other professionals.
- Before embarking on any of the above, talk to experienced teachers and get advice on how best to prioritize your workload. As we've said before, don't try to take on too much all at once.

Concluding discussion

In this book we have moved from considering the start of your teaching career, through the first term, first year and beyond to looking ahead to your future development as a more experienced teacher. As you can see from the last two chapters, there are many exciting and far-reaching developments and innovations in primary teaching at the moment, which will have an impact on all teachers' working lives and on the children whom they teach.

How you respond to these and other changes that will take place in the coming years depends on a number of factors. Earlier in the book, we looked closely at how Abbey, Cathryn, Fatou and Gina experienced their first years in teaching and saw how their developmental progress differed according to the schools they were working in as well as personal factors, such as family commitments, age and prior experience. For each of you there will be a similar set of factors which affect how well you develop professionally in your first years as a teacher. We have seen how important the school context is to this, particularly the quality of the school leadership and the support and guidance of more experienced teachers. We've also identified a number of obstacles or barriers that you may face in your early career.

The activities in each chapter have hopefully enabled you to think about yourself as a teacher and reflect on your own capabilities as well as to become more aware of the factors in your own situation that can help you develop or hold you back. Finally, we have given you some ideas about the way that you can continue to develop professionally, both within and beyond your own school. Remember, make the most of the opportunities and resources that are available to you, especially your colleagues.

Further reading and useful website links

Hargreaves, A. (2003) *Teaching in the Knowledge Society*. Buckingham: Open University Press.

MacGilchrist, B. and Myers, K. (2004) *The Intelligent School*, 2nd edn. London: Paul Chapman.

Middlewood, D., Parker, R. and Beere, J. (2005) *Creating a Learning School*. London: Paul Chapman.

Also see

DfES (2004a) *Every Child Matters: Next Steps*. London: DfES. www.everychild matters.gov.uk

National Remodelling Team at www.remodelling.org

The National College of School Leadership at www.ncsl.org.uk/networked _learning

And information about new developments in extended schools at www.teachernet. gov.uk/extendedschools

Appendix

In this appendix details of the three main studies which underpin this book are presented.

Study 1: the preparedness and professional development of beginning primary teachers

The initial part of this study was funded by the Economic and Social Research Council (ESRC). The funded element was carried out between 2000–01, tracking groups of newly qualified primary teachers during the 18 months following their initial training (Griffiths et al. 2002). The non-funded element of the study was completed in 2005 and involved tracking four of these new teachers through their third and fourth years. (The whole study had been preceded by a pilot study which was conducted during 1998–2000 within one local education authority).

There were three main areas of investigation:

1 *Adequacy of preparation* for primary teaching: the extent to which newly qualified teachers were prepared to teach the whole primary curriculum and fulfil other professional responsibilities, and the gaps, if any, between initial training and professional requirements and needs.
2 The *types of support* given to beginning primary teachers during their early years in teaching.
3 *Professional development and learning*, including identification of patterns of transition from initial training to the first years of teaching and key factors which enabled or inhibited their professional development.

Research design and sample

The study consisted mainly of a survey of newly qualified teachers across three local education authorities (LEAs) and follow-up in-depth interviews with a sample of 34 teachers. Four of these teachers were tracked through to their fourth year and became case studies. Data were collected by the following means:

1   Initial questionnaires to 270 primary newly qualified teachers during their second term in teaching. Completed questionnaires were returned by 129 NQTs (response rate 48 percent). Of these 117 were women, 11 men and 1 respondent did not state whether they were male or female. Many had trained on an undergraduate route (82 out of the 129 respondents) and most of the respondents (123 out of the 129) were below 40 years of age.

2   Follow-up telephone interviews with 34 NQTs (31 women, 3 men) which represented 26 percent of the respondents to the initial questionnaire. These interviews were carried out towards the end of their first year in teaching. The sample of new teachers covered a cross-section of age, gender, type of training, type of school (rural/urban, size, age-phase, etc.), prior work experience and specialist key stage across the three local education authorities and were chosen from those who indicated on the questionnaire their willingness to be further involved in the study.

3   Second questionnaires to 270 primary NQTs towards the end of their first year and beginning of their second year in teaching. Completed questionnaires were returned by 47 NQTs (response rate 17 percent).

4   Follow-up telephone interviews with the 34 NQTs (see 2 above) at the beginning of their second year in teaching.

5   Additional interviews were conducted with the four case study teachers in their fourth year of teaching.

6   Interviews with 12 school-based mentors, four from each of the three LEAs.

7   Interviews with advisors responsible for primary NQTs from the three LEAs.

Research methods

Questionnaires

The initial questionnaire asked the new teachers about:

- *general information*: their gender, age, qualifications and what they did before they trained as a primary teacher.
- *preparation for curriculum areas and wider aspects of school life*: the subject areas and aspects of school life in which they felt well prepared and less well prepared.
- *Career Entry Profile*: how their career entry profile had been used.

- *support: the type of support* they were given by the school and the LEA, and any other forms of support they found helpful.
- *the future*: where they saw themselves in five years' time.

The second questionnaire asked the new teachers about:

- *development of subject areas and wider aspects of school life*: the subject areas and aspects of school life they considered they had developed most/least.
- *rewards and challenges*: which aspects of their work had been the most rewarding and which had been the most challenging.
- *initial training*: which aspects of their initial teacher training had been particularly helpful/not helpful, and what gaps they could identify.
- *areas for development*: their main priority for next year in relation to their professional development.
- *the future*: where they saw themselves in five years' time.

Interviews with beginning teachers
In many cases the interviews specifically followed up questionnaire responses. However, they also enabled the following:

- Clarification, expansion and explanation of questionnaire responses.
- Gathering of additional data.
- Reflection on their learning and experiences.
- Provision of actual examples of experiences which highlighted the nature of phenomena.
- Cross-referencing and validation of data.

Interviews with school mentors and LEA advisors
Interviews were designed to gather the perspectives of school mentors and LEA advisors on the preparedness and professional development of beginning teachers. The main areas covered were as follows:

- *Major strengths and weaknesses of NQTs*: in subject areas and the wider aspects of school life.
- *School/LEA role*: perceived and actual role in relation to the professional development of beginning teachers. Particular emphasis was placed on the support the school/LEA perceived that the beginning teacher required, as well as the actual support provided by the school/LEA.
- *Career Entry Profile*: how it had been used.

Study 2: recruitment and retention of primary teachers in relation to changing requirements for initial teacher education (ITE) and primary schools

This study was carried out between 1999–2002. The main objectives were to identify issues affecting both recruitment into teaching (i.e. following training) as well as retention. Both were explored in relation to changing requirements for initial teacher education and primary schools.

Research design and sample

The research was designed to follow up all primary teachers who had trained on a PGCE programme at one institution in the 1990s. Questionnaires were sent to 469 former trainee teachers who trained between 1991–99 (the interval between qualifying and completing the questions was, therefore, 1–9 years). Of these, 219 teachers (193 women, 26 men) were eventually tracked down. Follow-up in-depth interviews were held with 10 teachers, the sample chosen to include a range of year groups across the decade. In addition, 22 (out of 23) teachers who trained in 1997–98 were also interviewed. This latter group became a cohort in Study 3 below.

Research methods

Questionnaires
The questionnaires sought data on the following areas:

- the teachers' current jobs and teaching careers (including any further training they had had);
- how well prepared they had felt on entering the profession;
- where they saw themselves in five years' time.

Separate sections for those who had left the profession and those who had never taught explored the following:

- reasons why they had left or not entered teaching;
- factors which could have encouraged them to enter or remain in teaching;
- factors which might encourage them to consider entering or returning to teaching in the future.

Interviews
Interviews were designed to explore similar areas as in the questionnaire. However, as with the interviews with beginning teachers (see Study 1 above), they were also designed for the gathering of additional and explanatory data.

Study 3: the cohort study

This study was funded by the ESRC. The three main areas of investigation were as in Study 1 above.

Research design and sample

In-depth telephone interviews were carried out in the spring term 2001 with 22 (21 women, 1 man) primary teachers who had qualified from a primary PGCE course in July 1998, i.e. in their third year of teaching. As in Studies 1 and 2, interviews were designed to explore areas covered in the questionnaire, along with additional and explanatory data relating to their first three years of teaching.

Bibliography

Alexander, R., Rose, J. and Woodhead, C. (1992) *Curriculum Organisation and Classroom Practice*. Oxford: Blackwell.

Altrichter, H., Posch, P. and Somekh, B. (1993) *Teachers Investigate their Work: An Introduction to the Methods of Action Research*. London: Routledge.

Audit Commission (2002) *Recruitment and Retention: A Public Service Workforce for the 21st Century*. London: Audit Commission.

Audit Commission/Ofsted (2002) *Recruitment and Retention of Teachers and Head-teachers: Strategies Adopted by LEAS*, HMI 709. London: Ofsted. (E-publication at www.ofsted.gov.uk)

Berliner, D.C. (1987) Ways of thinking about students and classrooms by more and less experienced teachers, in J. Calderhead (ed.) *Exploring Teachers' Thinking*. London: Cassell.

Black, P. and Wiliam, D. (1998) *Inside the Black Box: Raising Standards through Classroom Assessment*. www.kcl.ac.uk/depsta/education/publications/blackbox.html (accessed 29 July 2005).

Black, P., Harrison, C., Lee, C., Marshall, B. and Wiliam, D. (2003) *Assessment for Learning. Putting it into Practice*. Buckingham: Open University Press.

Blandford, S. (2000) *Managing Professional Development in Schools*. London: Routledge.

Bubb, S. and Earley, P. (2004a) *Leading and Managing Continuing Professional Development: Developing People; Developing Schools*. London: Paul Chapman.

Bubb, S. and Earley, P. (2004b) *Managing Teacher Workload*. London: Paul Chapman.

Calderhead, J. (1988) *Teachers' Professional Learning*. London: Falmer.

Calderhead, J. and Shorrock, S. (1997) *Understanding Teacher Education: Case studies in the Professional Development of Beginning Teachers*. London: Falmer.

Clandinin, D. J. (1986) *Classroom Practice: Teacher Images in Action*. London: Falmer Press.

Clarke, S. (2001) *Unlocking Formative Assessment: Practical Strategies for Enhancing Pupils' Learning in the Primary Classroom*. London: Hodder and Stoughton.

Cordingley, P., Bell, M., Rundell, B., Evans, D. and Curtis, A. (2003) *The Impact of Collaborative CPD on Classroom Teaching and Learning: How Does Collaborative Continuing Professional Development (CPD) for Teachers of the 5–16 Age Range Affect Teaching and Learning?* Review conducted by the CPD review group. London: EPPI-Centre, Social Science Research Unit, Institute of Education. http://eppi.ioe.ac.uk/EPPIWeb/home.aspx?page=/reel/review_groups/CPD/review_one.htm (accessed 20 July 2005).

Cowley, S. (2001) *Getting the Buggers to Behave.* London: Continuum.

Craft, A. (2000) *Continuing Professional Development.* London: RoutledgeFalmer with Open University Press.

Dalgety, Hutchings and Ross (2003) *Teacher Retention in Seven Local Education Authorities 2001–02.* London: Institute for Policy Studies in Education, London Metropolitan University.

Dean, J. (2004) *The Effective Primary School Classroom.* London: RoutledgeFalmer.

DfEE (Department for Education and Employment) (1998) *The National Literacy Strategy: Framework for Teaching.* London: DfEE.

DfEE (Department for Education and Employment) (1999) *The National Numeracy Strategy: Framework for the Teaching of Mathematics from Reception to Year 6.* Cambridge: Cambridge University Press for DfEE.

DfES (Department for Education and Skills) (2003a) *Every Child Matters: Green Paper.* London: HMSO.

DfES (Department for Education and Skills) (2003b) *Excellence and Enjoyment: A Strategy for Primary Schools.* Nottingham: DfES publications.

DfES (Department for Education and Skills) (2004a) *Every Child Matters: Next Steps.* London: DfES.

DfES (Department for Education and Skills) (2004b) *Primary Strategy Learning Networks.* London: DfES.

DfES/TTA (Department for Education and Skills/Teacher Training Agency) (2003) *Qualifying to Teach: Professional Standards for Qualified Teacher Status and Requirements for Initial Teacher Training.* London: TTA.

Drake, P., Jacklin, A., Robinson, C. and Thorp, J. (2004) *Becoming a Teaching Assistant.* London: Paul Chapman.

Dreyfus, H.L. and Dreyfus, S.E. (1986) *Mind Over Machine: The Power of Human Intuition and Expertise in the Era of the Computer.* Oxford: Basil Blackwell.

Elbaz, F. (1983) *Teacher Thinking: A Study of Practical Knowledge.* London: Croom Helm.

Eraut, M. (1994) *Developing Professional Knowledge and Competence.* London: Falmer Press.

Eraut, M. (2002a) Editorial, *Learning in Health and Social Care*, 1(4): 178.

Eraut, M. (2002b) Editorial, *Learning in Health and Social Care*, 1(1): 4.

Eraut, M. (2004) Informal Learning in the Workplace, *Studies in Continuing Education*, 26(2): 247–73.

Fielding, M. (ed.) (2001) *Taking Education Really Seriously: Four Years' Hard Labour.* London: RoutledgeFalmer.

Fielding, M. and Bragg, S. (2003) *Students as Researchers: Making a Difference.* Cambridge: Pearson Publishing.

Fielding, M., Bragg, S., Craig, J. et al. (2005) *Factors Influencing the Transfer of Good Practice,* research report no. 615. London: DfES.

Flutter, J. and Rudduck, J. (2004) *Consulting Pupils. What's in it for Schools.* London: RoutledgeFalmer.

Fullan, M. and Hargreaves, A. (1992) *What's Worth Fighting for in Your School? Working Together for Improvement.* Buckingham: Open University Press.

Furlong, J. and Maynard, T. (1995) *Mentoring Student Teachers: The Growth of Professional Knowledge.* London: Routledge.

Furlong, J., Barton, L., Miles, S., Whiting, S. and Whitty, G. (2000) *Teacher Education in Transition: Re-forming Professionalism?* Buckingham: Open University Press.

Gipps, C., Hargreaves, E. and McCallum, B. (2020) *What Makes a Good Primary School Teacher?* London: RoutledgeFalmer.

Goodson, I. (ed.) (1992) *Studying Teachers' Lives.* London: Routledge.

Griffiths, V., Jacklin, A. and Robinson, C. (2002) *Investigating the Preparedness of Newly Qualified Primary Teachers.* ESRC end of award report R000223489.

GTC (General Teaching Council) (2002) *Teachers on Teaching: A Survey of the Teaching Profession.* London: GTC.

GTC (General Teaching Council) (2005) *Teacher Learning Academy* http:// www.gtce.org.uk/cpd_home/TLA/ (accessed 25 July 2005).

Hargreaves, A. (2003) *Teaching in the Knowledge Society.* Buckingham: Open University Press.

Hargreaves, A. and Fullan, M. (1992) *Understanding Teacher Development.* London: Cassell.

Hargreaves, A. and Fullan, M. (1998) *What's Worth Fighting for in Education?* Buckingham: Open University Press.

Hart, S., Dixon, A., Drummond, M.J. and McIntyre, D. (2004) *Learning Without Limits.* Buckingham: Open University Press.

HoC (House of Commons) Education and Skills Committee (2004a) *Secondary Education: Teacher Retention and Recruitment,* 5th report of session 2003–04, Vol. 1. London: HMSO.

HoC (House of Commons) Education and Skills Committee (2004b) *Secondary Education: Teacher Retention and Recruitment,* 5th report of session 2003–04, Vol. 2. London: HMSO.

Hoodless, P., Bermingham, S., McCreery, E. and Bowen, P. (2003) *Teaching Humanities in Primary Schools.* Exeter: Learning Matters.

Howson, J. (2001) Forsake history but don't leave maths in the lurch, *Times Education Supplement,* 20 April.

Huberman, M. (1993) *The Lives of Teachers.* London: Cassell.

LCC (Leicestershire County Council) (2003) *Recruitment and Retention Resources for Schools and Colleges.* www.leics.gov.uk/index/education/support_for_schools/recruitment_retention/ (accessed 23 February 2005)

Leat, D. (undated) *Partnership and Participation in Teacher Research.* Cranfield: National College for School Leadership, Cranfield University.

LeCompte, M. and Preissle, J. (1993) *Ethnography and Qualitative Design in Educational Research,* 2nd edn. London: Academic Press.

Levinson, D.J. (1978) *The Seasons of a Man's Life.* New York: Knopf.

Lewis, A. and Lindsay, G. (eds) (2000) *Researching Children's Perspectives.* Buckingham: Open University Press.

MacGilchrist, B. and Buttress, M. (2004) *Transforming Learning and Teaching.* London: Paul Chapman.

MacGilchrist, B. and Myers, K. (2004) *The Intelligent School,* 2nd edn. London: Paul Chapman.

Middlewood, D., Parker, R. and Beere, J. (2005) *Creating a Learning School.* London: Paul Chapman.

Moor, H., Halsey, K., Jones, M. et al. (2005) *Professional Development for Teachers Early in their Careers: An Evaluation of the Early Professional Development Pilot Scheme,* research report no. 613. London: DfES.

Moyles, J. and Robinson, G. (eds) (2002) *Beginning Teaching: Beginning Learning.* London: Open University Press.

Muijs, D. and Reynolds, D. (2005) *Effective Teaching,* 2nd edn. London: Sage.

Ofsted (2002) *The Curriculum in Successful Primary Schools,* HMI:553. London: Ofsted.

Ofsted (2003) *Teachers' Early Professional Development,* HMI: 1395. E-publication document (on website only) at: www.ofsted.gov.uk

Penny, S., Young, S., Ford, R. and Price, L. (2002) *Teaching Arts in Primary Schools.* Exeter: Learning Matters.

Pollard, A. (2002a) *Reflective Teaching: Effective and Evidence-informed Professional Practice.* London: Continuum.

Pollard, A. (2002b) *Readings for Reflective Teaching.* London: Continuum.

Pollard, A. and Bourne, J. (1994) *Teaching and Learning in the Primary School.* London: Routledge in association with the Open University.

PricewaterhouseCoopers (PwC) (2001) *Teacher Workload Study,* final report. London: PwC.

Roffey, S. (2004) *The New Teacher's Survival Guide to Behaviour.* London: Paul Chapman.

Rudduck, J. and Flutter, J. (2004) *How to Improve Your School.* London: Continuum.

Schon, D.A. (1983) *The Reflective Practitioner: How Professionals Think in Action.* London: TempleSmith.

Sikes, P., Measor, L. and Woods, P. (1985) *Teacher Careers: Crises and Continuities.* London: Falmer.

Simco, N. (2003) *Succeeding in the Induction Year,* 2nd edn. Exeter: Learning Matters.

Smithers, A. and Robinson, P. (2001) *Teachers Leaving.* Liverpool: University of Liverpool.

Smithers, A. and Robinson, P. (2003) *Factors Affecting Teachers' Decisions to Leave the Profession,* research report 430. London: DfES.

Smithers, A. and Robinson, P. (2004) *Teacher Turn-over, Wastage and Destinations.* London: DfES.

Stoll, L., Fink, D. and Earl, L. (2004) *It's About Learning (and it's About Time) What's in it for Schools.* London RoutledgeFalmer.

Sturman, A. (1999) Case study methods, in J.P. Keeves and G. Lakomski (eds) *Issues in Educational Research.* Oxford: Elsevier Science.

Sturman, L. (2003) *Contented and Committed? A Survey of Quality of Working Life Amongst Teachers.* Slough: NFER.

Teacher Support Network (2002) *The Secrets of Teacher Wellbeing: Teacher Support Network Conference: Retention in Schools,* 20 May. www.teachernet.gov.uk/teachingandlearning/library/retention/ (accessed 23 February 2005).

Thomas, G. (1992) *Effective Classroom Teamwork: Support or Intrusion?* London: Routledge.

Tomlinson, P. (1995) *Understanding Mentoring: Reflective Strategies for School-based Teacher Preparation.* Buckingham: Open University Press.

Torrance, H. and Pryor, J. (1998) *Investigating Formative Assessment.* Buckingham: Open University Press.

TTA (Teacher Training Agency) (2003a) *Induction Standards: TTA Guidance for Newly Qualified Teachers.* London: TTA.

TTA (Teacher Training Agency) (2003b) *Keeping Good Teachers: Effective Strategies in Teacher Retention.* London: TTA.

Vincent, K., Cremin, H. and Thomas, G. (2005) *Teachers and Assistants Working Together.* Buckingham: Open University Press.

Weston, C. (2004) *The Inclusive Classroom: A Practical Guide for Teachers.* Exeter: Learning Matters.

White, P., See, B. H., Gorard, S. and Roberts, K. (2003) *Review of teacher recruitment, supply and retention in Wales,* working paper no. 41. Cardiff: School of Social Sciences, Cardiff University.

Wolfendale, S. (1992) *Involving Parents in Schools.* London: Cassell.

Wood, E. and Attfield, J. (2005) *Play, Learning and the Early Childhood Curriculum.* London: Paul Chapman.

Yeomans, R. and Sampson, J. (1994) *Mentorship in the Primary School.* London: Falmer Press.

Zeichner, K.M. and Tabachnick, B.R. (1981) Are the effects of university teacher education 'washed out' by school experience? *Journal of Teacher Education,* 32(3): 7–11.

Zeichner, K.M., Tabachnick, B.R. and Densmore, K. (1987) Individual, institutional and cultural influences on the development of teachers' craft knowledge, in J. Calderhead (ed.) *Exploring Teachers' Thinking.* London: Cassell.

Index